W9-BEO-157

B 1430 02618408 7
a 31430025184087b
UNIV. OF MD. COLLEGE PARK

PICTURESQUE CALIFORNIA HOMES;

A VOLUME OF

FORTY PLATES, PLANS, DETAILS AND SPECIFICATIONS OF HOUSES

SAMUEL & JOSEPH C. NEWSOM, ARCHITECTS AND PUBLISHERS, { 504 KEARNY ST., SAN FRANCISCO, 1004 BROADWAY, OAKLAND, } CALIFORNIA.

ORIGINALLY PUBLISHED IN SAN FRANCISCO 1884

INTRODUCTION BY DAVID GEBHARD

HENNESSEY & INGALLS, INC. LOS ANGELES 1978

213/474-2541

Review copy
Retail price: $14.95
Publication date: Nov. 27, 1978

Hennessey & Ingalls, Inc.

Art and Architecture Books
10814 West Pico Boulevard
Los Angeles, California 90064

National Trust

for

Historic Preservation

Guarding   *America's Heritage*

N. T. H. P. Library
740 Jackson Place, NW
Washington, DC 20006

PICTURESQUE
CALIFORNIA HOMES.

ARCH
NTL
NA
7035
.C2 N72
19,78

PICTURESQUE CALIFORNIA HOMES;

A VOLUME OF

FORTY PLATES, PLANS, DETAILS AND SPECIFICATIONS OF HOUSES

COSTING FROM $700 TO $15,000,

AND ADAPTED TO FAMILIES HAVING GOOD TASTE AND MODERATE MEANS.

CITY AND COUNTRY HOMES.

SAMUEL & JOSEPH C. NEWSOM, ARCHITECTS AND PUBLISHERS

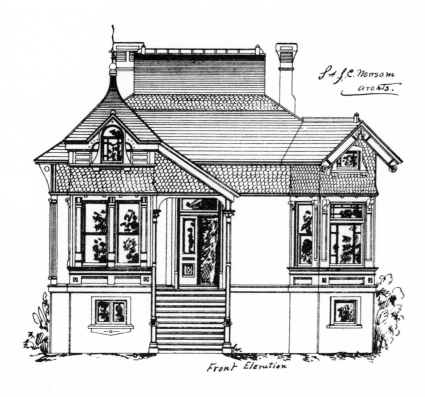

Front Elevation

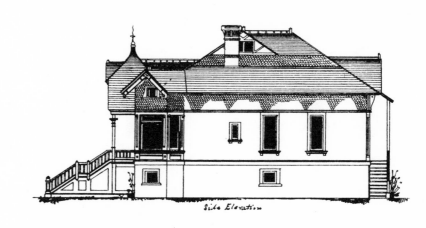

Side Elevation

ORIGINALLY PUBLISHED IN
SAN FRANCISCO 1884

INTRODUCTION BY DAVID GEBHARD

HENNESSEY & INGALLS, INC.
LOS ANGELES 1978

Library of Congress Cataloging in Publication Data

Newsom, Samuel.
  Picturesque California homes.

  Facsim. of v. 1 of the work published by the authors
in 4 v. in 1884.
  1. Architecture, Domestic—California.
2. Architecture, Victorian—California. 3. Dwellings
—California. I. Newsom, Joseph Cather, joint author.
II. Title.
NA7235.C2N472 1884a   728.3   78-4248
ISBN 0-912158-82-4

Introduction copyright ©1978 by David Gebhard
All rights reserved

Published by Hennessey & Ingalls, Inc.
8321 Campion Drive
Los Angeles, CA 90045

INTRODUCTION
DAVID GEBHARD

Throughout the eighteenth, the nineteenth and much of the twentieth centuries architectural pattern books have provided the designs for a majority of America's domestic buildings.[1] While some of these pattern books were essentially carpenter manuals addressed directly to the artisan, most were general plan books which were purchased as much by potential clients and literati as by carpenters and builders. By far the majority of these pattern books were published in New York, Boston, and Philadelphia, and as a general rule they were authored by individuals who considered themselves (and were considered) architects.[2] The typical format used throughout most of the nineteenth century was the division of these books into two sections of text. The first discussed the more abstract aspects of architecture — the need for responding to functional considerations, the desirability of designing buildings as art objects (i.e. of "elevating public taste"), the moral necessity of good architecture, and finally, in some volumes, the need for a national or "modern" style of architecture. The remaining text often considered specific architectural problems, ranging from landscaping and siting to structure and plumbing; this section usually included a text description of individual buildings with illustrations of them.

Especially difficult for the architect-authors and publishers of plan books were the decades from after the Civil War to the beginning of the First World War. These years witnessed an amazing and rapid sequence of architectural fashions. Some publishers of pattern books, such as George Evertson Woodward of New York, sought to solve this problem by continually issuing new books, each of which attempted to respond to the most recent change in taste.[3] Others, like Fred T. Hodgson of Chicago, simply retained older images and reused them again and again in new editions or under different titles.[4] But whether up to the latest trend or old fashioned and behind the times, these pattern books

1. See Helen Park, *A List of Architectural Books Available in America Before the Revolution* (Hennessey and Ingalls, Inc., Los Angeles, 1973); Henry Russell Hitchcock, *American Architectural Books* (new expanded edition), with an introduction by Adolf Placzek (Da Capo Press, New York, 1976); the influence of pattern book design in the nineteenth and twentieth centuries is discussed in David Gebhard and Deborah Nevin's *200 Years of American Architectural Drawings* (Whitney Library of Design, New York, 1977).

2. Hitchcock, *op cit.*, lists publishers and places of publication for pattern books published before 1895.

3. Hitchcock, *op cit.* (pp. 117-119), lists 20 volumes and/or new editions published by Woodward between 1865 and 1879. Another publisher whose books were extensively used was Palliser and Palliser of Bridgeport and New York. See Hitchcock, *ibid.*, pp. 75-76.

4. Fred T. Hodgson, *Modern Carpentry* (Frederick J. Drake and Co., Chicago, 1903); *A Practical Treatise on the Steel Square and its Application to Everyday Use,* in two volumes (Frederick J. Drake and Co., Chicago, 1903).

were all pervasive throughout the United States, with the result that towns and villages as well as the residential suburban areas of the larger cities were filled with houses derived from them. Both the rapid change in images on the one hand and the conservatism of domestic architecture on the other were to a large extent due to this extensive publishing effort.

One of the questions which often comes to mind during the perusal of these pattern books is why should an architect produce such a volume? What advantages did he feel he would gain as a professional? Generally the reasons for publishing such works were pretty much the same as those which prompted Andrea Palladio to publish his *Four Books of Architecture* in 1570, or Robert and John Adam to bring forth their three folio volumes in 1773, 1779, and 1822.[5] The publication of the work of an architect was in many instances a far more effective way of selling the architect and his product than an array of built buildings. It made it possible for him to reach a wider public. Furthermore, the presentation of drawings (and from the late nineteenth century on of photographs) alongside the printed word in a book helped associate architecture and the architect with the elite world of traditional humanism. In late nineteenth-century America the architect who authored a pattern book could create the illusion for himself and for his prospective clients that he was not just another local architect, but one of regional, if not national prominence and that he was a practitioner who would be able to bridge the gap between architecture as "art" and architecture as the practical down-to-earth business of producing buildings.

In a number of the pattern books published after 1875, the architect openly advertised that plans for the illustrated dwellings could be purchased for extremely reasonable sums. It would be fascinating to have an accurate count of how many plans of this type were actually purchased. The number was probably quite small and the drawings illustrated in these volumes were most likely used as a direct visual source by builder and client who thought it unnecessary to purchase a more complete set of drawings.

Not only do these pattern books provide us with a rich array of popular architectural images of the past, they also give us a clue as to how each period thought about (as well as looked at) visual forms. Thus, when a pattern book of the early 1880s mentions the Eastlake Style, or later the Queen Anne, we can gain at least some idea how the period responded to different images and why some were considered appropriate and others not. In addition to the question of images, these pattern books revealed the great importance that architects and clients placed on utilitarian matters, ranging from questions of structure and materials to "scientifically" designed kitchens, bathrooms, central heating and plumbing.

5. It was the plates of illustrations, not the texts, which were responsible for the widespread influence of both Palladio and the Adam brothers.

The cultural and business predominance of the Northeast meant that most pattern books were published in New York and sometimes in Boston and Philadelphia, but few in other parts of the country. It wasn't until Chicago emerged as a major urban environment in the late nineteenth century that very many pattern books were published outside the Northeast. Minneapolis and Kansas City became important publishing centers only after 1900, and on the West Coast Los Angeles eventually emerged (also after 1900) as a principal publication center for pattern books which advanced the cause first of the Craftsman bungalow and later, in the twenties, of the Spanish Colonial and other historic revivals.[6]

As with other far-away provincial areas, California and the West Coast brought forth only a few pattern books in the nineteenth century. Other than the illustrations contained in the *California Architect and Building News* (published in San Francisco between 1879 and 1899), it would seem that most domestic designs were derived from the eastern pattern books or from one or another of the eastern architectural periodicals.[7] It is difficult for us today to know which of these eastern pattern books were most extensively used in California. A probable hint is given from time to time in the pages of the *California Architect and Building News* where commercial advertisements for these books were presented. Several of Palliser and Palliser's volumes, including *Palliser's New Cottage Homes and Details* (1878 and later), *Palliser's Useful Details* (1881?), and *Palliser's American Architecture* (c. 1888), were advertised or mentioned in the *California Architect and Building News* between 1883 and 1899.[8] Other pattern books mentioned in this periodical were Charles D. Lakey's *Lakey's Village and Country Houses or Cheap Homes for all Classes* (1875), Daniel T. Atwood's *Atwood's Revised Rules of Proportions* (1892), and J.H. Kirby's *Hints on the Practical Construction of Dwelling Houses* (date?).[9]

There is no reason to think that the number of pattern books in use on the West Coast was limited only to these volumes. Others encountered in pre-1900 California architectural libraries were Samuel Sloan's *The Carpenter's New Guide* (1854); Henry W. Cleveland, William Backus and Samuel D. Backus's *The Requirements of American Village Homes* (1856); George Evertson and F.W. Woodward's *Woodward's Country Homes* (1865); and H. Hudson Holly's *Modern Dwellings in Town and Country* (1878). One of the most often

6. To date there is no compilation similar to Hitchcock's which covers American architectural pattern books published after 1895.

7. In addition to the *California Architect and Building News*, domestic designs were presented in *The Building News* (San Francisco), *The Architect and Builder* (San Francisco), *Architect, Builder and Mechanic of Southern California* (Los Angeles), and *Artistic Homes of California* (issued with the *San Francisco Newsletter*, F. Marriotta).

8. *California Architect and Building News*, Vol. 4, August, 1883, p. 139; *California Architect and Building News*, Vol. 20, March, 1899, p. iii.

9. *California Architect and Building News*, Vol. 3, February, 1882, p. 32; *California Architect and Building News*, Vol. 4, September, 1883; *California Architect and Building News*, Vol. 8, May 15, 1887, p. 60.

discussed volumes was Charles L. Eastlake's *Hints on Household Taste* (1852 and later); and there is every reason to believe that the illustrations contained in this volume were highly influential on the West Coast, especially from the late 1870s through the 1890s.[10]

San Francisco, as the chief city of the West Coast in the nineteenth century and a regional center, did produce a few pre-1900 pattern books. Of those, John Cotter Pelton, Jr.'s *Cheap Dwellings* (1880 and later) assumed the classic format of a pattern book.[11] A.J. Bryan's *Architectural Proportion* (1880) contains detailed drawings.[12] John Gash (who was at one time associated in partnership with John J. Newsom) discussed the relationship of the architect and builder in his *A Catechism of Architecture* (1893), and the San Francisco firm of Salfield and Kohlberg illustrated their own work in their *Modern Buildings of California* (c. 1890).[13] By the early 1900s a number of southern and northern California architectural firms had begun to publish books (or perhaps we should call them brochures) of their work.

Of all of the pattern books published during the late nineteenth century on the West Coast the most sumptuous were those published by the brothers Samuel and Joseph Cather Newsom, architects of San Francisco, Oakland and Los Angeles. The first of their famous pattern books was published either late in 1884 or early 1885.[14] It was titled *Picturesque California Homes* (San

10. "The 'Eastlake Style' of Architecture," *California Architect and Building News*, Vol. 2, October, 1881, p. 97; "Eastlake," *California Architect and Building News*, Vol. 3, March, 1882, p. 33; "The Circus Style," *California Architect and Building News*, Vol. 7, August 10, 1888, p. 114.

11. John Cotter Pelton, Jr., *Cheap Dwellings* was first reviewed in the *California Architect and Building News*, Vol. 1, December, 1880, p. 116. A smaller but similar volume was that of Frank L. Smith, *A Cozy House: How it was built* (Boston, 1887).

12. A.J. Bryan's *Architectural Proportions*, like a number of late nineteenth century volumes on California architecture, was published by the major San Francisco publishing house of Bancroft and Co.

13. John Gash, *A Catechism of Architecture* (William Doxey, San Francisco, 1893) was reviewed in *The Architect and Builder*, Vol. 1, November, 1894, p. 98; David Salfield and Herman Kohlberg's volume was mentioned in the *California Architect and Building News*, Vol. 11, December 20, 1893, p. 128.

14. None of the four Newsom volumes are dated. The first volume was issued either in late 1884 or during the first months of 1885. In "The Articles of Agreement," on pp. 2–6, the date June 15, 1884, is given. The D.H. Boyd House in Eureka, which is illustrated in the first volume in Pl. 14, was mentioned in the *California Architect and Building News*, Vol. 5, August, 1884, p. 154. In the "Preface" to Vol. 2 of the series the authors state that ". . . we, about two years ago, published a few plates — thirty-five in all — under the title of *California Homes, No. 1*." If the date of 1887 is correct for volume 2, then 1885 or early 1884 would be correct. The tentative dating of volumes 2, 3, and 4 is based upon notices of publication contained in the *California Architect and Building News*, the time periods during which the Newsoms occupied offices whose addresses are given in the volumes, the dating of buildings illustrated in the volumes, and information about individuals and firms who advertised in the volumes. Volume 2 of *Picturesque California Homes* presents Samuel and Joseph Cather Newsom's work entirely via drawings (as in the first volume). The last two volumes,

Francisco). This was followed in 1887 by *Picturesque California Homes No. 2* (San Francisco). Both of these volumes were jointly authored by the two brothers. In 1890 Joseph Cather Newsom published the third volume in the series, entitled this time *Picturesque and Artistic Homes and Buildings of California* (San Francisco); and in 1893 he published the last of the volumes, *Modern Homes of California* (San Francisco). Previous to No. 2 in the series, Joseph Cather Newsom published two other volumes. One of these, *Artistic Buildings and Homes of Los Angeles* (San Francisco, 1888), was devoted to work in the Los Angeles area. The other was a small volume, *California Low Priced Cottages* (San Francisco, 1888?), which illustrated single-floor and story-and-a-half cottages for northern and southern California.

In 1890 Samuel Newsom published a number of designs under the title *Some City and Suburban Homes* (San Francisco).[15] At the end of the decade, during his stay in Philadelphia, Joseph Cather Newsom gathered together a variety of his own and other designs, and published them in a series entitled *Up-To-Date Architecture* (Philadelphia, 1898). While in Philadelphia, J. Cather also published a group of designs of churches under the title *New Booklet on Churches* (Philadelphia, c. 1898). Thus between them, the two brothers ended up in publishing at least eight pattern books between late 1884 and 1898, and in addition they saw many of their designs published in the pages of the *California Architect and Building News,* the *Architect and Builder,* the *Architect and Engineer, The Architect's Directory, Scientific American Builder's Edition, The Inland Architect,* etc.

The Newsoms, as individuals or in partnership, were among the most prolific nineteenth-century West Coast architectural firms. Examples of their town plans as well as residential, commercial and institutional buildings were to be found throughout the length and breadth of California. At one time, in the 1880s, they actively maintained offices in San Francisco, Oakland and in Los Angeles. Though we will never possess anything approaching a complete record of their work (built and unbuilt), it is likely that they realized over 600 buildings in the state.

The brothers Samuel (1852-1908) and Joseph Cather Newsom (1858-1930) received their architectural training through the traditional nineteenth century apprenticeship method. Four of the brothers within the Newsom family became practicing architects in California. These four, John J., Thomas D., Samuel and Joseph Cather, were born in Canada, near Montreal.[16] Their father, uncle

authored by Joseph Cather Newsom alone, employ both drawings and photographs. The last two volumes are more complex to follow since a number of the buildings illustrated are not by Joseph Cather Newsom but by other architects. These architects are mentioned in the "Introduction," but the specific buildings are not credited.

15. Joseph Cather Newsom, *Artistic Buildings and Homes of Los Angeles* (Britton and Rey, San Francisco, 1888); Samuel Newsom, *Some City and Suburban Homes* (Bancroft and Co., San Francisco, 1890).

16. According to Samuel Newsom (Jr.), John Newsom, the eldest son of Lavens Newsom "... was a graduate of Montreal College (Canada) and taught his

and oldest brother John J. Newsom came to San Francisco in 1860 (?) and were followed by the rest of the family in 1861 (?). Their father Lavens M. Newsom, while occasionally involved in building, was primarily a horticulturist. During his later life he operated a nursery in Oakland. The two older brothers John J. and Thomas D. formed an architectural firm, Newsom Brothers, in San Francisco at the beginning of the 1870s.[17] Samuel Newsom worked as a draftsman in this firm through 1873. Between 1874 and 1876 he listed himself as an architect, and through 1878 he was associated with his older brothers. In 1878 Samuel formed a partnership with his younger brother Joseph Cather Newsom, and it was this famous and productive partnership which was to last through 1888. Joseph Cather, like his brother Samuel, had gained his architectural experience primarily in the office of his two older brothers.

By the mid 1880s the firm of Samuel and Joseph Cather Newsom (sometimes labeled Newsom and Newsom, or Newsom Brothers, to help confuse the historical picture) had emerged as a major California firm. They then had offices in San Francisco and Oakland, where they both continued to live, and they were producing buildings throughout the whole of northern California. Though they did produce schools, business blocks, factories, warehouses and multiple housing, their real forte was residential architecture, and particularly speculative single family housing. It was during this period that they designed their most famous house, the William Carson House in Eureka (1884), and in the same year issued the first of their pattern books.

With their business interest in speculative housing, they found the intensive boom of the late 1880s in Southern California too strong a temptation to resist. In 1886, Joseph Cather went south and opened a branch office of the firm in Los Angeles. The decision to open an office in Los Angeles was highly advantageous, for the Newsom's shortly found themselves designing a number of substantial business blocks, large upper-middle class dwellings, and "spec" housing. They also became closely involved in the design and layout of a number of the new boom towns of the 1800s such as San Dimas and Pacoima. In addition, the firm provided these towns with designs for speculative housing and the plans for a hotel, which like the shopping center of today was the major come-on attraction.

In January, 1888, the firm was dissolved with Joseph Cather remaining in Los Angeles and Samuel "retaining control of the San Francisco office."[18] The Los Angeles office continued to be highly

brothers Samuel, Joe and Thomas architecture in his office." Letter from Samuel Newsom (Jr.) to David Gebhard, dated October 2, 1970. Like their younger brothers, John J. and Thomas D. Newsom also published a small pattern book which contained their own designs and the designs of other West Coast and non-West Coast architects. This volume was entitled *Up to Date Residences* (Brown, Meese, Craddock, San Francisco, 1897?).

17. See the *Oakland City Directory,* between 1870 and 1873.

18. *California Architect and Building News,* Vol. 9, January 15, 1888, p. 12.

productive through 1889, but by 1890 with the end of the boom, building opportunities pretty well ceased in the Southland. In 1891, Joseph Cather returned to the Bay Area and established an office in San Francisco. At the end of the 1890s and again in the early 1900s he was associated with Samuel and Sidney, but these proved to be short-lived partnerships. In 1897 he left the Bay area with his family to work in Philadelphia (1897-99?). He returned to Oakland and San Francisco in 1900, and remained there through early 1903.[19] In 1903 he was again listed as an architect practicing in Los Angeles. He remained in Los Angeles from 1903 through 1905, and he went back once again to San Francisco and Oakland where he continued to practice through the early 1920s.[20]

Samuel Newsom is somewhat easier to follow for he remained in the Bay area where he always maintained a San Francisco office. From 1888 through 1898 he practiced independently; in 1899 he formed a partnership with Frederick H. Meyer which lasted through 1900. In the late 1890s his son Sidney, who had been working as a draftsman for his father, became a partner. He was later joined by his younger brother Noble Newsom, and the firm of Newsom, Newsom and Newsom continued until Samuel's death in 1908.[21]

As architects both of the Newsom brothers were highly competent. Their buildings were carefully and well planned in a utilitarian sense — including practical planning, well thought out structural detailing, and the latest in heating, plumbing, kitchen and bathroom layouts. As to imagery and imaginative spatial planning, the Newsoms were obviously closely aware of the changes in fashion which were so rapid during these years. Their earliest work could be characterized as loosely Eastlake, which was followed by designs in all of the major styles of the 80s, 90s and early 1900s — the Queen Anne, Richardsonian Romanesque, the Chateauesque, and the Colonial Revival Shingle style. By the early 90s, Samuel and Joseph Cather became interested in designing in the regionally developed Mission Revival style. Later came designs which indicate an interest in the Spanish Colonial Revival and even the Pueblo Revival. Side by side with designs employing these regional images, they created others which were classical and Beaux Arts, Gothic and English Tudor, and after 1900 often Craftsman — bungalow and late Shingle style.

19. Letter of S.D. Nelson to David Gebhard concerning his grandfather Joseph Cather Newsom (dated June 24, 1971).

20. William T. Comstock, *Architect's and Specification Index for 1905-06* (William T. Comstock, New York, 1905), p. 25. Joseph Cather Newsom was listed as working and living in the Bay Area through 1897; he was then not listed again until 1901. He remained listed in Oakland through early 1903; and he is then not encountered in the Bay Area until 1907. In 1910 he formed a brief partnership with I.E. Frary. From 1914 on he was sometimes listed as an architect, at other times he was listed as a real estate promoter or salesman.

21. See Samuel Newsom's obituary in the *Architect and Engineer,* Vol. 14, September, 1908, p. 79.

Certainly one of the remarkable qualities of these designers is how difficult it is to distinguish the work of one brother from the other. There is no reason to doubt that the Southern California work was primarily produced by Joseph Cather, but we cannot say with any degree of certainty whose hand predominated in the pre-1886 work. Equally intriguing is the similarity in their work after they separated in 1888. There is very little to distinguish an 1890s or early 1900s Mission Revival or Colonial Revival design of Samuel from that of his brother.

Though they kept up with the latest styles, the buildings of each exhibit recognizable jointly shared personal qualities which distinguished their work from their contemporaries. Perhaps the most telling element in their work was the peculiar way in which they mixed and maneuvered their details and forms. They both seem to take a delight in seizing upon a detail and then enlarging it, or miniaturizing it, and then posing it not as an integrated feature of a design but as a separate, highly individual historic fragment. From beginning to end their designs were (from the point of view of sophisticated academic architecture) an affront. There was always something bizarre — and therefore delightful and playful — about their buildings. For the trained architect or critic, their designs are almost always outrageous, and yet the outrageousness is so appealing that we tend to be won over.

This sense of outrage is evoked most forcefully by the buildings themselves, but it also can arise from a look at the drawings in their pattern books. The predominant style in the first volume is the Queen Anne. Their interpretation of this style can be seen in the Rosenthal House in San Francisco of 1884 (pl. 34), or in the more modest Davisson House (pl. 1) of the same year in Oakland. Their wildest and most adventuresome excursions into the Queen Anne are contained in their project for a "Picturesque Cottage" (c. 1884) (pl. 3); their large Picturesque Country Residence (c. 1884) (pl. 15); and their Summer Residence (c. 1884) (pl. 18) at Santa Rosa. Their designs of a few years earlier, like the Helmrich House in San Francisco (1881) (pl. 16) or the groups of three cottages illustrated in pl. 29, are Eastlake with a slight touch of the Queen Anne.

In their earlier designs, such as that for the Hirsfeld House (pl. 35), they openly referred to themselves as "Eastlake architects." With regard to imagery, the most advanced design in the first volume is the Queen Anne Shingle style house (c. 1884) illustrated in pl. 11. But a careful look at each of these designs will aptly demonstrate how the Newsoms provided highly rational plans and combined these with the most erratic use of visual historic fragments.

The 35 plates contained in Volume One of *Picturesque California Homes* contain drawings for 37 dwellings and cottages. Of these, 19 are for individual houses which were built.[22] It is likely that the remaining 18 designs were produced for specific projects or were "spec" plans which the architects hoped would be used by investor-builders. Of the houses illustrated in this volume two are still in excellent condition. These are the Boyd House (pl. 14) of 1884-85 in Eureka (northeast corner of 4th and Myrtle Streets), and the Swett House (pl. 25) of 1883 in Stockton (143 W. Acacia Street).[23]

The following list is of the 19 designs which were built:

The plates of drawings in the first volume of the Newsoms' pattern books are large in size when compared to the usual format size of most pattern books of the 1880s and 1890s. With the one exception of the drawing of the Evans Cottage (pl. 24), all of the plates of drawings follow the conventional arrangement of providing a front and side elevation, and one or more floor plans. Occasionally drawings of details are also provided — ranging from gable ends to railings, staircases, doors, mantels, wainscotting, etc. All of the drawings are provided with a scale, and the plans give their basic dimensions. Certain designs are further described by the inclusion of a vertical cut-away wall section which gives the height of each floor.

Each of the floor plans is reasonably descriptive, indicating such features as fireplaces, gas outlets and the principal fixtures for the kitchen and bath. The floor plans together with the elevational drawings present a reasonably accurate picture of the exteriors of the buildings.

These elevational drawings rely exclusively on line to describe the basic form of a building, all of its details, and its many different tactile surfaces. Shading, as an effective drawing technique, is not present, and indications of the site and landscape are at best cursory.

The drawings are technically adequate and pretty well mirror the quality found in the average architectural publications of the period. They convey, to be sure, a self-taught atmosphere, which indicates that neither brother was academically trained in rendering. As long as they relied on the instruments of the drafting board, all went well, but when they were faced with trying to use those instruments to indicate an angular projection (like a bay or tower) their descriptive powers usually failed. Still there was a close relationship between these drawings conditioned by the drafting board, and the surface and details of their built buildings conditioned by the jigsaw and lath.

---

22. The dating of these houses is based upon construction notices published in the *California Architect and Building News* and other building records.

23. The locations of other still standing buildings (1978) designed by the Newsoms are listed in David Gebhard, *A Guide to Architecture in San Francisco and Northern California* (Peregrine Smith, Salt Lake City, 1972) and David Gebhard and Robert Winter, *A Guide to Architecture in Los Angeles and Southern California* (Peregrine Smith, Salt Lake City, 1977).

PICTURESQUE CALIFORNIAN HOMES;

A VOLUME OF

FORTY PLATES, PLANS, DETAILS AND SPECIFICATIONS OF HOUSES

COSTING FROM $700 TO $15,000,

AND ADAPTED TO FAMILIES HAVING GOOD TASTE AND MODERATE MEANS.

CITY AND COUNTRY HOMES.

It is designed to meet the wants of that large number of persons who have but a limited amount of money at their command, and in building a home wish to use it to the best advantage.

Mechanics, clerks, salaried men, workingmen of every calling, carpenters and builders in cities, towns and villages, will find this book a useful aid, worth many times its cost in the information and practical suggestions which it gives.

SAMUEL & JOSEPH C. NEWSOM, ARCHITECTS AND PUBLISHERS, { 504 KEARNY ST., SAN FRANCISCO, 1004 BROADWAY, OAKLAND, } CALIFORNIA.

DESCRIPTION OF PLATES:

Burglar and Fire-Proof Vaults and Safes, DOORS, SHUTTERS, House and Cemetery Railings, Stairs, etc.

H. & J. RALSTON,

Manufacturers of all kinds of

Architectural and Ornamental Iron Works

151 & 153 Beale Street, Corner of Howard, SAN FRANCISCO.

Jobbing attended to with Dispatch. Country Orders promptly executed.

ARTICLES OF AGREEMENT, Made this *fifteenth* day of *June*, one thousand eight hundred and eighty-*four*, BETWEEN *John Smith*, of the first part, and *John Jones*, of the second part:

1st.   The said party of the second part, does hereby, for *himself*, *his* heirs, executors and administrators, covenant, promise and agree with and to the said party of the first part, *and his* executors, administrators and assigns, that *he*, the said party of the second part, *and his* executors and administrators, shall and will, for the consideration hereinafter mentioned, on or before the *tenth of August*, well and *sufficiently* erect and finish the Building *of a dwelling* conformable to the Drawings and Specifications made by *S. & J. C. Newson*, Architects, and signed by the parties and hereunto annexed, within the time aforesaid, in a good, workmanlike and substantial manner, to the satisfaction and under the direction of the said *S. & J. C. Newsom*, Architects, to be testified by a writing or certificate under the hand of the said *S. & J. C. Newsom*, Architects, and also shall and will find and provide such good, proper and sufficient materials of all kinds whatsoever as shall be proper and sufficient for completing and finishing all the *carpenter, etc.*, and other works of said Building mentioned in the *general* Specification, for the sum of *Five Thousand* Dollars, in lawful money ; AND the said party of the first part does hereby, for *himself and his* heirs, executors and administrators, covenant, promise and agree, with and to the said party of the second part, *and his* executors and administrators, that *he*, the said party, of the first part, *and his* executors or administrators, shall and will, in consideration of the covenants and agreements being strictly performed and kept by the said party of the second part, as specified, well and truly pay, or cause to be paid unto the said party of the second part, *and his* executors, administrators or assigns, the said sum of *Five Thousand* Dollars in gold Coin, lawful money of the United States of America.

IN THE MANNER FOLLOWING:

NOTE.—*(Payment to be made to suit both parties.)*

Provided, that in each of the said cases a certificate be obtained and signed by the said *S. & J. C. Newsom, Architects.*

AND IT IS HEREBY FURTHER AGREED BY AND BETWEEN THE SAID PARTIES :

FIRST.—The Specifications and Drawings are intended to co-operate, so that any works exhibited in the Drawings and not mentioned in the Specifications, or vice versa, are to be executed the same as if it were mentioned in the Specifications and set forth in the Drawings, to the true meaning and intention of the said Drawings and Specifications.

SECOND.—The Contractor, at his own proper costs and charges, is to provide all manner of materials and labor, scaffolding, implements, moulds, models, and cartage of every description, for the due performance of the several erections.

THIRD.—Should the owner, at any time during the progress of said building, request any alterations, deviations, additions or omissions from the said Contract, specifications or plans he shall be at liberty to do so, and the same shall in no way affect or make void

the contract, but will be added to or deducted from the amount of the said contract price, as the case may be, by a fair and reasonable valuation.

FOURTH.—Should the contractor, at any time during the progress of said works, refuse or neglect to supply a sufficiency of materials or workmen, the owner shall have the power to provide materials and workmen (after three day's notice in writing given) to finish the said works, and the expenses shall be deducted from the amount of the said contract price.

FIFTH.—Should any dispute arise respecting the true construction or meaning of the Drawings or Specifications, the same shall be decided by *S. & J. C. Newsom*, and their decisions shall be final and conclusive; but should any dispute arise respecting the true value of the extra work or works omitted, the same shall be valued by two competent persons—one employed by the owner and the other by contractor—and in case they cannot agree, these two shall have power to name an umpire, whose decision shall be binding on all parties.

SIXTH.—The owner shall not in any manner be answerable or accountable for any loss or damage that shall or may happen to said works, or any part or parts thereof respectively, or for any of the materials or other things used and employed in finishing and completing the same (loss or damage by fire excepted)...............

IN WITNESS WHEREOF, the said parties to these presents have hereunto set their hands and seals, the day and year first above written.

Signed and sealed in the presence of⎫ *John Smith*, [Seal.]
 P. Hays,   ⎬ *John Jones.* [Seal.]
 H. Martin.   ⎭ ....[Seal.]

BOND.

KNOW ALL MEN BY THESE PRESENTS : That we, *John Jones*, as principal, and *W. Johnson*, surety, of *San Francisco*, California, are held and firmly bound unto *John Smith*, of *same place*, in the sum of *One Thousand* dollars, in lawful money of the United States of America, to be paid to the said *John Smith & his* executors, administrators or assigns ; for which payment well and truly to be made, we bind ourselves and each of our heirs, executors and administrators, jointly and severally, firmly by these presents. Sealed with our seals, and dated the *fifteenth* day of *June*, one thousand eight hundred and eighty-*four.*

The condition of the above obligation is such, that whereas, the above bonded *John Jones* has entered into a written contract with the above named obligee, *John Smith*, to build for *him* a *dwelling* on *his* lot on *Fourth* street and *Mission*, in the *City of San Francisco*, County of *San Francisco*, State of California, for the sum of *Five Thousand* dollars, in gold coin of the United States of America, according to plans and drawings and specifications made and prepared by *S. & J. C. Newsom*, architects.

Now, therefore, if the said *John Jones* shall fulfill his said contract, in strict conformity with the terms of *his* said contract, plans and specifications, and shall well and truly pay all bills and claims

for labor performed or material furnished, for and in the construction and carrying out of said building, and shall protect and hold harmless the said *John Smith* from any and all claims or liens filed or recorded against said building, and lot or premises whereon the same or any part thereof shall be erected ; also shall protect and hold harmless the said *John Smith* from all costs, counsel fees or damages by reason thereof, then the above obligation to be void, otherwise to remain in full force and virtue.

Signed, sealed and delivered in the⎫
  presence of   ⎬ *John Jones,* [Seal.]
 P. Hays,
 H. Martin.   ⎭ *W. Johnson.* [Seal.]

Dated June 15th, 1884.

SPECIFICATIONS

FOR THE LABOR, MATERIALS, AND MECHANICAL WORKMANSHIP REQUIRED FOR THE ERECTION AND COMPLETION OF

....

To be situated on Fourth street and Mission, in the City of San Francisco, County of San Francisco, State of California, for *John Smith*, owner, and according to the drawings made for the same by *S. & J. C. Newsom*, Architects.

For a more particular description of the work, see the drawings, which are to be considered with, and made a part of these specifications.

MATERIALS, CONDITIONS, ETC.

All timber (except otherwise specified) to be Oregon Pine, the best quality, well seasoned.

All lumber (except otherwise specified) to be Redwood, the best quality, well seasoned.

All Doors and Sash to be of Sugar Pine, the best quality, well seasoned, made in the best manner.   Drawers and Shelves of.........

All the materials of their several kinds to be the best quality ; the work to be done in the most thorough and workmanlike manner, in accordance with the plans, whether original or detail, prepared by *S. & J. C. Newsom*, and in accordance with these specifications, under the superintendence, and to the entire satisfaction of the said *S. & J. C. Newsom.*

Upon completion, the buildings to be cleared of all rubbish, thoroughly and neatly swept ; the premises cleared of all refuse, and every part and portion of the work to be in perfect order upon delivery and acceptance. (*Windows to be cleaned after completion.*)

The owner reserves the right to reject any or all bids for the work.

Should the contractor introduce any materials different from the sort and quality herein described, or meant to be implied, it shall be immediately removed at the contractor's expense, at any time during the progress of the work, and inside of 24 hours.

The contractor to give his personal superintendence to the work ;

to furnish all transportations, labor, materials, scaffolding and utensils needful for performing the work in the best manner, according to the plans and specifications and details.

No part of the work to be sub-let, unless by consent of the architects and owner.

DRAINS.

To be Iron Stone, 6 inches, with branches 5 inches, well laid, joints to be cemented with Portland cement, and fall to be at least ¼ inch to one foot, to have y's, turns, traps, etc., to be at least 18 inches below lot surface, to connect with sewer in street—if none, to be connected with cesspool; all to be laid where shown, or so as to connect with all waste pipes and conductors.

Cast Iron Drain Pipe, to be 4″ and 2″ inches in diameter, joints to be thoroughly water-tight, with y's, turns, and traps, etc., open trapped Hoppers to same, where shown on plans.

EXCAVATIONS.

Clear away all rock, dirt, or rubbish necessary to leave the site for the intended building clear and unencumbered, and excavate for footings of walls and piers, as shown by the drawings, to firm and solid grounds. Footings of walls to be not less than 6 inches below the finished level of lot grade. Dig the bank well away from the walls and leave the same open until the walls are well set and dry.

GRADING.

Fill in around and pack the earth against the brick walls after the mortar is dry, and level it with the bottom of the underpinning.

Grade the excavated earth around and slope off the ground on all sides of the building as directed, and remove all surplus earth from off the premises.

CHIMNEYS.

Build the chimneys to correspond with the drawings, and in no case allow more than four inches in thickness for brickwork between timber or any woodwork and the smoke flues. All the smoke flues to be 8x8, straight and true. Smoothly parguetted partitions in flues to be 4 inches thick, built into top of each chimney, outside walls of each chimney to be 4 inches in thickness, and built as shown by the drawings. Top out above the roofing, using hard burned picked brick for facing, laid in white mortar, in accordance with the design and detail drawings, and properly cleaned down at completion.

All fire-places lay up in the ordinary manner for coal-set grates and the proper size to suit the same. Build proper ledges in throats of fire-places for dampers.

Turn trimmer arches under all hearths.

Put ash pit dump grates of iron to the fire-places where ash pits are provided under. Place iron bars ½ by 3 inches in arches, also over ash pits as required for carrying same, and turn a relieving arch over same; furnish an iron frame, properly walled in place to each ash pit, these to have iron doors hung and secured in appropriate manner as directed.

Furnish, and set in the brickwork of flues for stove-pipes, proper cast-iron stove collars and thimbles where required; also provide the necessary bricks, mortar, etc., for setting mantels and range.

BRICK WORK.

Use good, sound, hard, well burned brick throughout, which must be well wet before being laid, with flushed solid joints. All brick to be laid up in the best and most workmanlike manner, with mortar composed of good Santa Cruz lime and clean, sharp sand, in proper proportion to make satisfactory mortar. All brick walls to be made perfectly level and straight to the proper and exact height, and to a true line from one end to the other.

Build brick piers inside and outside as shown on drawings. Turn trimmer arches for the support of all hearths at the time chimneys are built.

The brick work to be well bedded, flushed and tied in every sixth course and worked in regular bond. Set properly all door and window frames in brick work. Underpin all sills with suitable mortar after the walls are up. Provide the needful materials of every description, and cover the walls from the weather at all necessary times. Attend other mechanics when required to back in and fill up properly behind their work.

Wall to be 18 inches high and 9 inches thick, and to have footings 17 inches wide.

Basement walls to be 24 nches high, 9 inches thick, and to have footings 17 inches wide.

HEIGHT OF STORIES.

Basement	6 feet 5 inches
First story	12 feet inches
Second story	11 feet 6 inches

SIZE OF TIMBERS, ETC.

Wall caps.	2	inches x	8	inches,	redwood
Main sills and trimmers	6	" x	6	"	pine
Plates	2	" x	4	"	"
Studs below main sills	4	" x	4	"	redwood
And at the corners	4	" x	6	"	"
Braces at foundation	3	" x	4	"	"
Joists, 1st tier, "bridged in solid at ends"	2	" x 10		"	pine
Joists, 2d tier	2	" x 12		"	"
Basement joists	2	" x	6	"	redwood
Ceiling joists	2	" x	6	"	pine
Rafters	2	" x	4	"	"
Studs	2	" x	4	"	"
All corners, doors and windows to be doubled	4	" x	4	"	
Except some closet partitions may be	2	" x	3	"	"
Bridging and bracing above main sills 2 inches x 3 inches, and	2	" x	4	"	"
Side strips to carry the joists	1	" x	4	"	"
Studs and joists	16 inches between centers				
Rafters	2 feet 8	"	"	"	
Studs in foundations	2 feet 8	"	"	"	
Rafters well supported over partitions.					

All timber below the main sills to be the best heavy redwood, ground sills or wall caps to rest upon a good solid basis, and well rammed down. The main sills (and trimmers) properly halved together; the main sills to run across the building as well as lengthwise.

The entire foundation, as well as the whole frame, to be *thoroughly braced and strongly nailed.*

SIZE OF TIMBER, ETC.

Joists around stairs, fire-places, chimneys, etc., to be doubled and framed together in the best manner; both tiers of joists to have two rows each of herring bone, 2x3 cross bridging, well cut and nailed in. Partitions to have suitable sills and plates, and all to be well bridged once around in each story. The entire frame to be thoroughly braced in all partitions, independent of the bridging, and strongly nailed. All doors and windows to have suitable strong headers, as directed.

The carpenter to do all the furring required to make all ready for the lather; also to cut away and make good before and after the gas-fitter and plumber. *All corners to be studded or furred solid before lathing.* Angle studs backed up with inch Oregon pine, strongly nailed on.

ROOF.

To have gutters arranged to carry the water off at one or more corners as directed, through 2½ inch diameter outlets and conductors; the roof to be boarded open joints, and deck close joints, with good, sound, inch rough Oregon, well nailed to every rafter; and make all ready for the shingling, which will be done with 16″ sawed redwood shingles, laid 4″ to the weather; joints well broken; 2 nails to each shingle.

Fancy Shingles—Where and as shown.

VENTILATORS, Fancy Cast Iron.

To be of 12 inches x 16 inches, to be put where directed or shown, 6 in all.

RUSTIC AND SHEATHING.

Enclose the whole outside with ⅞x8″ redwood V rustic, well seasoned; best quality; well nailed to every stud; laps to be painted; every butt joint to be painted; butt joints to have a 3x11-inch piece of tin to keep out the water.

STEP LADDER

Of Oregon pine, neatly made, dressed, and painted, where directed —to be used for access to roof.

SCUTTLE.

In size and position as directed; well hung with wrought-iron strap hinges; fastened with strong hooks, staples and chain, complete for use.

FRONT STEPS

Will be substantially and neatly built upon suitable stringers; risers of inch stuff; treads of 1⅜″ Oregon pine stuff; nosings rounded; rail 10 inches high, neatly moulded and capped; pedestals 10 inches x 10 inches, moulded base and moulded cap; make, hang, and trim a batten door under front steps for access to the gas meter closet. Enclose under steps with rustic.

REAR STEPS

Will be built upon strong stringers, inch risers, and one and three-fourths inch treads, nosings rounded, filling under rail, 2″ balusters.

FRONT ENTRANCE.

The recess will be floored 6 inches below main floor, with tongued and grooved Oregon; no piece to be more than 3 inches wide, put together with lead and oil; the vestibule paneled and moulded to match the door.

EXTERIOR

Will be finished as per "Elevation" and "Details," which will be given.

ANGLE BEEDS

Of white pine for all fire-places and chimney corners, and all other corners similarly exposed.

VERANDAH

Will be well timbered; floored same as front porch; sealed overhead with 1x4 R. W.; the roof boarded for shingling or tinning.

FLOORS

Will be laid of Oregon pine, the best quality, well seasoned, ⅞″x4″, dressed, tongued and grooved, laid in courses, joints neatly evened and cleared off, closely and carefully driven up, blind-nailed on every joint, in the tongued edge, and also nailed down through the ploughed edge to every joist, with suitable floor brads to prevent warping; taking care all round to shut out rats and mice. No floors to be laid until the roof is on, unless otherwise instructed by the Architects.

INSIDE BLINDS.

The windows in all rooms where marked I B on plans to have inside blinds of cedar, to be made in folds about 8 inches wide, and cut at meeting rails; to be hinged with 2½ inch brass butts, to have 1¼ brass flaps, and to have suitable shutter knobs, and trimmed and finished complete . . . .

OUTSIDE BLINDS.

All the windows of the building where marked O B to have outside blinds in two folds 1¼ inches in thickness, with rolling slats, to be properly hung with cast-iron hinges, and secured with the most approved fastenings to keep open or shut.

SASH, GLASS, ETC.,

To be made of best, clear, dry white pine, unless otherwise specified; with acorn mold sash-bar, weather-lipped meeting rails; to be double hung with pleated sash cord and iron weights; to be 1½ inches thick.

Single sash of basement windows, to be hung with butts, and to have the necessary fixtures to securely shut or keep out.

Glass—The glass in basement 16 ounce.

Glass in first and second story to be crystal sheet, 21 ounce.

The glass in hall windows to be plain cathedral.

The glass in front door transoms to be ornamented cathedral, to cost $25.

The glass to be well bedded, tacked and puttied.

Panel Backs—The windows in all main rooms to have panels under sills, formed as shown by drawings. Stools to balance of house.

CRESTINGS

To be of iron to cost 50 cents per foot.

Posts $1 each.

FINIALS

To be as per drawings.

DOORS.

All doors, except those specified different, to be made of clear, dry white pine, free from sap and double-faced throughout, and must be in strict accordance with the drawings, of mouldings, etc., and to have hard pine saddles throughout.

The principal story outside doors to be of clear and dry white pine, made as per drawings.

For the thickness, height and width of doors see plans.

Hanging.—Hang all doors throughout with loose joint butts of sufficient size to throw them clear of architraves. All doors over seven feet high to have three butts each.

1st story butts to be of enameled iron to be 4½″ x 4½″ in size.
2d story   "   "   "   "   "   "   "

Sliding Doors.—To run on heavy, polished brass track, laid perfectly level on floor, to have four-inch patent slot sheaves and nickel-plated iron stop in center, at top; double doors to have astragal joint in center. . . . .

Knobs and Escutcheons.—Front main entrance doors to have bronze knobs on both sides to have bronze trimmings. All other doors throughout to have knobs, to cost $5 per dozen. Double doors to have a knob to each fold, if desired. Sliding doors to have flush handles. Put suitable knobs on all dwarf doors, press doors, etc., as directed; also, on shutters. Drawers to have pulls of Berlin bronze.

Locks.—The main entrance doors to have six-inch mortise locks with four keys; to have bronze fronts and striking plates, to cost $8.

First floor to have a first quality four-inch mortise lock, brass fronts and striking plates, to cost per doz. $12. Sliding doors to have locks with astragal fronts of brass and flush furniture.

All presses, drawers, etc., to have suitable locks as approved.

Sash Locks.—Every double hung window in the building to have the Morris Burglar-proof Sash Lock on meeting rail, to be of Berlin bronze.

Sliding Bolts.—Double doors to have flush sliding bolts at top and bottom, and to correspond with other furniture.

Hardware to cost $ . . . . . . (Hardware to be paid for by contractor;) to be selected by architects. Contractor to furnish specified list of same to the architects when required.

INSIDE FINISH.

All jamb-casings proper width to receive the lath and brown mortar; door-jambs 1½ inch thick (excepting front door-jambs, which will be 2 inches thick), Oregon pine.

SASH STOPS,

Or beads, inside at the sides of all windows, to be fastened in with raised head silver-headed screws.

FACE CASINGS.

Those in all rooms and halls to be 6 inches wide, and 1⅛ inches thick; open architrave; with suitable plinths; all as per details.

NOTICE.

No inside finish to be put on until the last coat of plastering is on.

All interior woodwork to be finished up perfectly clean, to be hand-smoothed and sand-papered, and at completion to be properly cleaned, and all stains and finger-marks removed off of such work as requires finishing in natural manner.

BASE.

In all rooms and halls 10 inches wide, besides the moulding; properly moulded on top.

WASH BASINS

Will be neatly finished up, enclosed underneath with inch tongued and grooved stuff, no piece more than 3½ inches wide, and to have neat panel door, well hung and trimmed with brass fastening and Berlin bronze knob.

KITCHEN AND PANTRY

Will be neatly ceiled all around three feet high (and 24 inches higher over the sink) with narrow inch tongued and grooved red-wood, beaded, capped with nosing and scotia; no piece more than 3½ inches wide.

SINK.

The sink to be neatly enclosed underneath, properly capped, and have a batten door well hung and fastened with good loose butts, brass facings, and Berlin bronze knob.

CLOSETS

Will be fitted up with shelves and hooks complete, as directed; to be arranged, as to size and position, as directed by the architects.

CHINA CLOSET.—To be fitted up with counter shelf about two feet eight inches high, and with shelves above placed on movable strips, so they may be adjusted to any height; below counter shelf put in three drawers with pulls, etc., complete, as directed.

STAIRS.

MAIN STAIRCASE.—To be built as shown by the floor plans, in the best and most substantial manner, to be properly supported and rough bracketed; to have one inch riser, 1⅜ inch tread, tongued and grooved together and both housed into wall-string; rise and tread to be as per figures on floor plan, fractions and variations in building excepted. Treads to have nosings with fillet and cove under, and the finished work of stairs to be put after plastering is finished and dry; wall-strings to be 1⅛ inches, top edge moulded to correspond with adjoining base; front string and landing facias to be finished with Oregon pine and redwood, worked and moulded as per drawings, and the space or wall under front string to be enclosed with plaster, as shown by the drawings. Stairs to be of clear, dry Oregon pine.

NEWELS, RAILS AND BALUSTERS.—To be as per details, and to be of selected dry Walnut. The hand-rail to be closely bolted at the joints, and to all posts, newel, etc.; all to be properly and well secured. Newell 8x8 inches in size in one solid piece; no glueing or staving up will be allowed, unless paneling is required. Posts 6x6 inches in size, solid, with cut work, etc., and tops finished as shown; ceiling drops and lower edge of facia finish to be as per drawings. Baluster filling between rail and string to be turned, framed and fitted together in manner as shown by the drawings.

Rear stairs as directed.

WATER CLOSET IN BASEMENT OR ON PORCH,

To be located as drawn or as directed, three feet by six feet, and eight feet high in the clear, between floor and ceiling, floored with inch tongued and grooved stuff, boarded up and down, all around and overhead with narrow tongued and grooved inch redwood, dressed. The door two feet six inches by six feet ten inches, one and one-half inches thick, two panels with slat panel above, cased with an opening over it for light. Door to be well hung with loose butts, and well trimmed with good rim lock and knobs. Put in a suitable riser and seat, with the openings to have lids hung and clamped; the seats and lid to be of white pine. To have two lids.

MANTELS.

Furnished by owner.

KITCHEN PANTRY

Will be fitted up and furnished with shelves and hooks complete, as directed, and put in bins or drawers, to be located and arranged, as to size and position, as may be directed by the architects and owner,

as the work progresses, and be properly cased and trimmed, so as to work properly in their places.

Panel slide between China closet and pantry properly trimmed.

BATH ROOM

Will be ceiled all around five feet high, with narrow inch tongued and grooved stuff, joints beaded, capped with nosing and scotia, and to have neat base no piece more than 3½ inches wide; the tub to be neatly encased and capped; the capping of Walnut; the work properly fitted to plumbing work; and to put up shelves and hooks as may be required. Water closet to be fitted up in Walnut and screwed together.

PANEL WAINSCOTING in dining room to be four feet high, to be paneled with ten-inch panels, to have neat cap and base, and to be as per drawings.

WASH TUBS

Are to be made of white pine planks, 2 inch bottom and sides, 1½ inch ends and divisions let into sides, put together with white lead and linseed oil, each tub to have a separate cover 1¼ inch stuff well hung and clamped.

LATHING.

All walls, partitions, ceilings, and work that is furred or studded throughout the entire building to be lathed with sound lath, of full thickness, laid on a full three-eighths of an inch apart, with four nailings to the lath, and joints broken every twelve inches; under no circumstances must lath stop and form a long, straight, vertical joint, nor any lath put on vertically to finish out to corners or angles; neither must there be any lath run through angles and behind studding from one room to another; all angles to be formed and nailed solid (by carpenter) before or while the lathing is being done.

PLASTERING.

All walls, partitions and ceilings throughout the entire building to be plastered one good coat of brown well haired mortar, made of pure unslacked lime, and clean, sharp sand, free from loam and salt, and best cattle hair, to be thoroughly mixed by continued working and stacked in the rough for at least eight days before putting it on. To be properly put on and applied with sufficient force to secure strong clinches; straighten and float up the brown coat, and make it true at all points.

FINISH OF WALLS.

Cover all the brown mortar with a good coat of best white hard-finish, unless otherwise specified, composed of finishing lime-putty and plaster of Paris, and clean washed sand; mix them in proper proportions so as to secure a good, handsome and workmanlike job.

CENTER PIECES AND BRACKETS.

Put up neat and appropriate center-pieces in all rooms and halls where shown, to cost $20, as selected by the architects.

Walls to be straight and plumb, and even with the grounds; all angles to be sharp and regular in form.

PLASTER CORNICES, ARCHES, ETC.

Run around the ceilings of the rooms where shown a plaster stucco cornice, in size twelve inches on side wall, twelve inches on ceiling, of such style as shown by details.

PAINTING.

Furnish all materials and perform all labor for the full completion of proper painting of the building. The material and labor to be of the best description.

Cover all sap, knots etc., of woodwork with a good coat of strong shellac before priming; putty up all the woodwork smoothly after priming, also before applying last coat.

Paint the exterior dressed woodwork two good coats of best white lead and linseed oil in the following colors:

EXTERIOR.

Body on the work as directed.
Blinds—Inside, to be shellacked two coats.
Blinds—Outside, to be painted two coats same color as house.
Chimney tops, painted two coats and striped.
Front Doors and other outside Doors—To be painted three coats, and grained walnut, and varnished one coat with Hueter Bro's & Co's Wearing Body Varnish.
Roof to be painted two coats Prince's Metallic.
Paint all tin work two coats of Prince's Metallic or Pacific Rubber Metallic; leaders two coats the same.

INTERIOR.

STAIR RAIL AND BALUSTERS AND NEWEL to be filled with Wheeler's Wood Filler properly applied, rubbed and cleaned off when wet, and to be finished with two coats of shellac and rubbed down with pumice-stone and oil to a dead and even surface.

All other woodwork on interior, not otherwise specified, to have three good coats of best white lead paint as directed. Grain the woodwork in all rooms, halls and vestibules in imitation of oak and walnut and finish with one good coat of Hueter Bro's Elastic Copal Varnish, and then waxed one coat.

The painter must see that all the woodwork is perfectly clean before filling; putty up all nail heads and other defects, using care to thoroughly match the putty in all hard wood and natural wood finish, and to sand-paper smooth and properly prepare all work before applying the second coat. All graining work to be of the best kind, and the whole of the painter's work to be done in the best and most thorough workmanlike manner known in the painting and finishing trade, and all paint and varnish spots to be cleaned off glass, walls and floors at the completion of the work, and all left in a perfect and complete state without exception.

GAS FITTING.

The gas pipes are to be laid according to the rules and regulations of the......Gas Company, for lights at places (on side wall and ceiling) where directed or marked G on the plans. The supply pipe to start at the proper place for the gas meter. The work to be done with the best material, in the most thorough and workmanlike manner, and to the satisfaction of the architects. Gas Inspector's certificate to be furnished to owner.

PLUMBING.

The water pipes to supply the premises to be of galvanized iron (excepting that suitable lead pipes are to be run of sufficient strength, of proper size, the best quality, where good work cannot be done with iron); all fittings to be galvanized; also, the escape pipe from the boiler to above the tank. The supply pipes, as well as all hot and cold water pipes on the premises to be $\frac{3}{4}$ inch in diameter (excepting the risers from the floor up may be $\frac{1}{2}$ inch); $\frac{1}{2}$ inch compression hose cocks to supply cold water in front and rear yard.

TANK.

To be 75 gallons capacity; cooper made; of $1\frac{1}{2}$ inch redwood properly ironed; the cover $1\frac{1}{8}$ thick, secured with clasps and staples, to have an eight-inch copper ball, $\frac{3}{4}$ inch cock; ball properly chained; $1\frac{1}{2}$ inch standing overflow and plug; all pipes, cocks, connections, etc., to make all ready and complete for use.

BOILER.

To be 40-gallon copper boiler, on Lockwood's iron stand; and with sediment cock, and all necessary connections.

SINK.

To be of steel, galvanized, 30"x32". To have 2 inch inside diameter cast iron waste pipe, and 2 inch Bower's trap and trap screw under the sink; $3\frac{1}{2}$ inch brass strainer, $\frac{3}{4}$ inch finished nickel compression cocks, with cast brass flanges; hot and cold water supply.

Sink to be lined up the back with zinc, nailed with brass nails.

SLOP HOPPER.

To be Burr's No. 1 Slop Hopper, properly connected to the sewer with three-inch pipe; water supplied from $\frac{3}{4}$ inch brass compression hose cocks.

WASH TRAYS.

To have hot and cold water supply, and $\frac{3}{4}$ finished brass compression tray cocks, with cast brass flanges; and a $1\frac{1}{2}$ inch cast iron waste pipe, with Bower's trap; brass strainers, plugs and chains.

WASH BASINS.

To be fourteen inches diameter, and to have $1\frac{1}{2}$ inch diameter (E) lead waste and overflow; $1\frac{1}{2}$ inch Bower's ball trap and trap screw under each basin; marble tops to fit the positions; back and sides to have O G moulded edges; marble $1\frac{1}{4}$ inches thick; backs

10 inches and $1\frac{1}{4}$ inches thick; to have medium size Fuller's compression cocks for hot and cold water; metal strainer plug; chain and chain stay; furniture all silver plated; basins clamped to the slabs with metal clamps.

BATH TUB.

To be lined with No. 11 zinc, and to have $1\frac{1}{2}$ inch diameter (E) lead waste and overflow Bower's (trap); brass strainer; plug and chain; and chain stay, hot and cold fullers, combination compression cocks, with hose and sprinkler; furniture all silver plated.

WATER CLOSET IN BASEMENT.

To be Sack's, with silver-plated cups and pull; 4 inch cast iron trap; cast iron soil pipe 4 inches in diameter; supply pipe to closet to be $\frac{3}{4}$ inch; soil pipe to be extended above the closet and out through the roof; the extension to be made of cast iron, same diameter as soil pipe.

SACK'S WATER CLOSET.

To be put in bath room, with pull handle act, complete according to instructions with each closet.

SAFES.

Of 6 lb. sheet lead, under sink, bath tub, wash basins, water closets, etc., edges turned up two inches and well tacked on the wood work all round; to have $\frac{3}{4}$ lead wastes, discharging outside; under tank to be the same.

WASTE PIPES.

All waste or soil pipes to be connected with the sewer; see that there are Y's, T's, or elbows, as may be most proper to make the required connection, and cement the joints in a thorough manner; extend the soil or waste pipes above the basins, sinks, bath tub, wash trays or water closets, etc., out through the roof. Same size as pipe.

All pipes to be neatly and properly fastened to the walls or ceilings; all joints to be wiped.

TINNING.

Valleys.—Line all valleys properly, and run the tin up under the shingles at least 10 inches. Tin work of valleys to be soldered in rosin.

Conductors.—Put up where indicated on plans the necessary number of galvanized iron conductors, with all necessary curves, bends, breaks, etc., to convey the water from the gutter to the grade level, and there connect them with the drain-pipe in the ground, and where there is no sewer connection to have suitable shoes on the bottom to throw the water from the building. All joints to be lapped and soldered tightly together; secure conductors to the building with galvanized iron fastenings, and place a wire screen over openings in gutters. All breaks and bends to be made and curved on a proper, neat and close sweep around the set-offs and breaks of the building, and all elbows to be made in like manner. (This is where they are exposed.)

The size of the conductors to be $2\frac{1}{2}$", to be run as directed.

Window Caps, Scuttle.—To be tinned with I. C. Tin.

Valleys.—To be lined with I. C. Tin.

Chimneys.—To be properly flashed with I. C. Tin flashings.

All Decks to be Tinned with I. C. Tin.

Flashings.—Furnish the carpenter all necessary painted tin flashings to enable him to flash all side wood work, casings, shingle work, wood cant boards, caps, etc., to make perfect and thoroughly tight work.

Where tin work of roofs comes against building, the tin must be run up at least six inches behind the rustic; also do all tinning requisite to make all places water tight, whether specified or not; go over the work and stop all leaks after other craftsmen, and leave everything tight.

All tin flashings to have two good coats of paint; the valleys and gutters to have two good coats of paint on under side before being used or laid; also to be painted on top on such portions as wood work or roof covering will lap on—this painting to be done by tinner with metallic roof paint.

Speaking Tubes.—Furnish and fit up with mouth-pieces and whistles complete—and prove them tight—the following speaking tubes:

From kitchen to where shown on plans by (S. T.)

ELECTRIC BELLS.

Provide and fit up in complete working order electric bells from kitchen to where marked on plans by (E. B.) different parts of the building, as directed; to have the necessary wires, buttons, and a suitable battery. Annunciator to be placed in kitchen, to be properly secured to wall, and to be of approved style and make, the whole to be warranted for two years.

Witnessed by...... { ....[Seal.]
{ ....[Seal.]
{ ....[Seal.]

Dated ...., 188

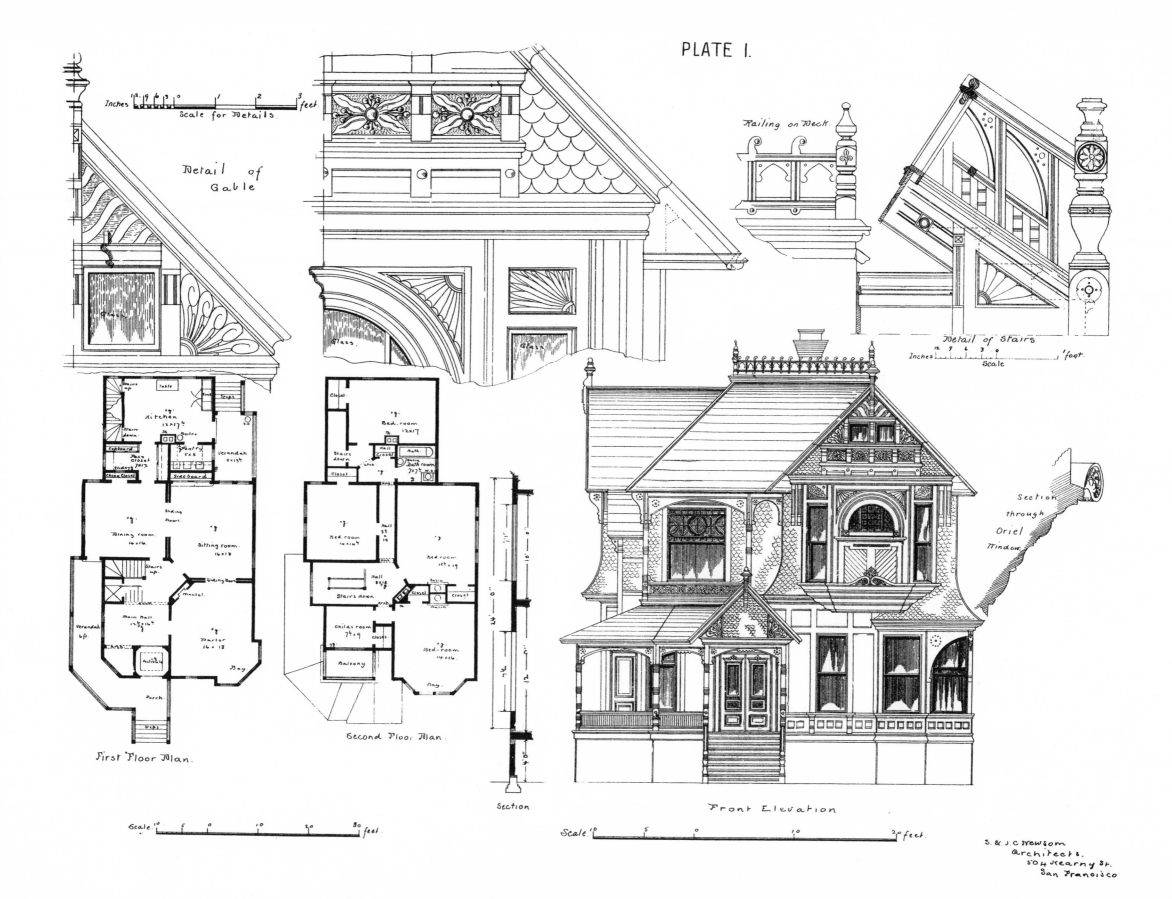

PLATE I.

Scale for Details

Inches 12 9 6 3 0   1   2   3 feet

Detail of Gable

Railing on Deck

Detail of Stairs
Inches 12 9 6 3 0   1 foot
Scale

Section through Oriel Window

First Floor Plan.

Second Floor Plan.

Section

Front Elevation

Scale 1 0   5   10   20   30 feet

Scale 1 0   5   0   10   20 feet

S. & J. C. Newsom
Architects.
504 Kearny St.
San Francisco

PLATE 2.

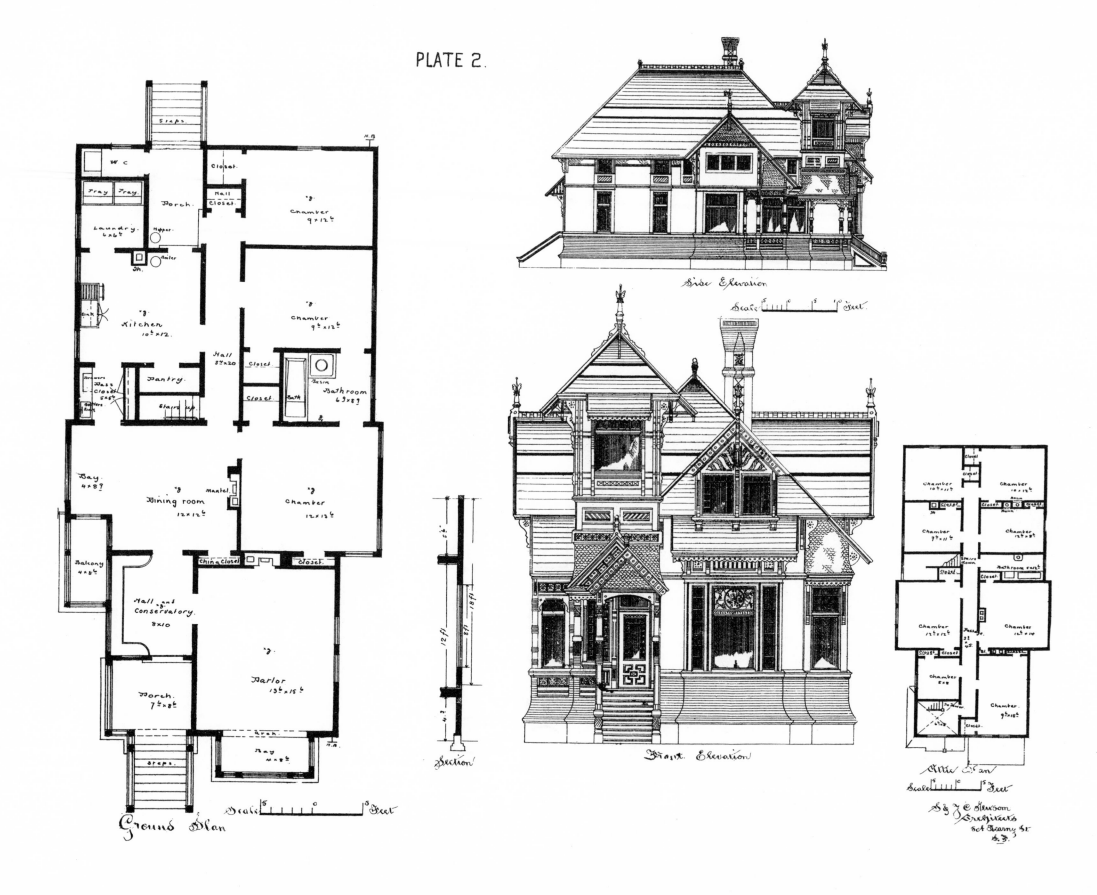

Side Elevation

Scale 5 5 10 Feet

Section

Front Elevation

W C

Closet
Hall Closet

Chamber
9×12⁶

Tray Tray
Porch

Laundry
6×6⁶ Hopper
Boiler
Th.

Chamber
9⁶×12⁶

Sink

Kitchen
10⁶×12

Hall
3⁶×20 Closet
Bath
Bath room
6⁶×8⁶
Basin

Drawers
Wash
Closet
5×5⁶
Gutters
Floor

Pantry

Stairs up

Closet

Bay
4×8⁶

Dining room
12×12⁶ mantel

Chamber
12×13⁶

Balcony
4×8⁶

China Closet Closet

Hall and
Conservatory
8×10

Parlor
13⁶×15⁶

Porch
7⁶×8⁶

Arch.

Bay
6×8⁶

steps

Ground Plan

Scale 5 5 Feet

Chamber
10⁶×11 Closet

Chamber
10⁶×11⁶ Basin
Closet

Chamber
9⁶×11 Closet

Chamber
12⁶×8⁶

Closet

Bath room bath
Closet

Chamber
12⁶×12⁶ Passage
3⁶×4⁵ Chamber
12⁶×14

Closet Closet

Chamber
6×8

Chamber
9⁶×12⁶

Attic Plan

Scale 5 5 Feet

S & J C Newsom
Architects
504 Kearny St
S.F.

PLATE 3

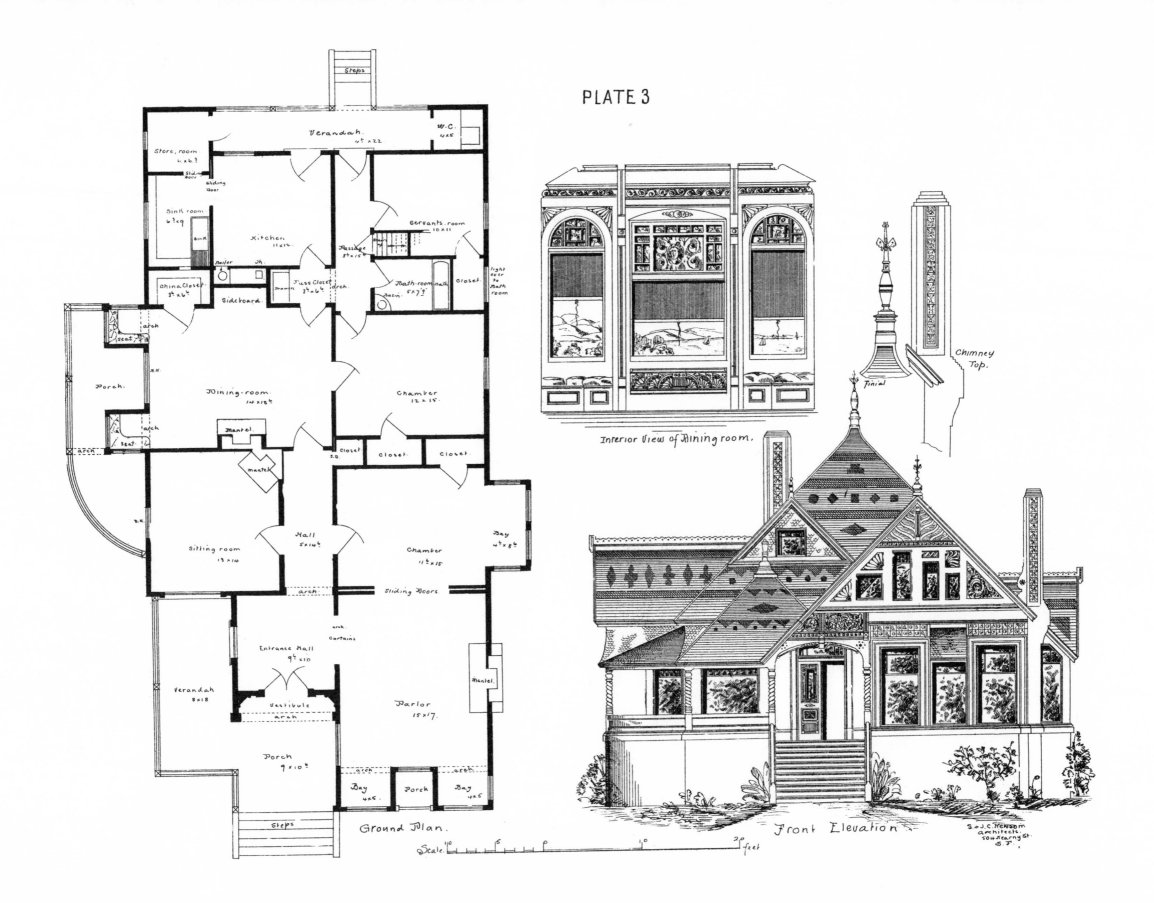

Verandah. 4' x 22

W.C. 4 x 8

Store room 4 x 6'²

Sliding Door

Sliding Door

Sink room 6'² x 9

Sink

Kitchen 11 x 12

Servants room 10 x 11

Passage 8' x 15

Boiler

J.h.

Press Closet 3' x 6'²

China Closet 3' x 6'²

Sideboard

arch

drawers

Bath room bath 5 x 7'²

Closet

light over to Bath room

basin

arch

seat

Porch.

A.H.

arch

seat

Dining room 14 x 18'²

Chamber 12 x 15

arch

Mantel

mantel

B.H.

Closet S.D.

Closet

Closet

Sitting room 13 x 14

Hall 5 x 14'²

Chamber 11'² x 15

Bay 4'² x 8'²

arch

Sliding Doors

arch

curtains

Entrance Hall 9' x 10

mantel

Verandah 8 x 18

Vestibule arch

Parlor 15 x 17

Porch 9 x 10'²

arch

arch

Bay 4 x 5

Porch

Bay 4 x 5

Steps

Ground Plan.

Interior View of Dining room.

Finial

Chimney Top.

Front Elevation.

S. & J. C. Newsom Architects. 304 Kearny St. S.F.

Scale 10   5   0   10   20   feet

PLATE 4

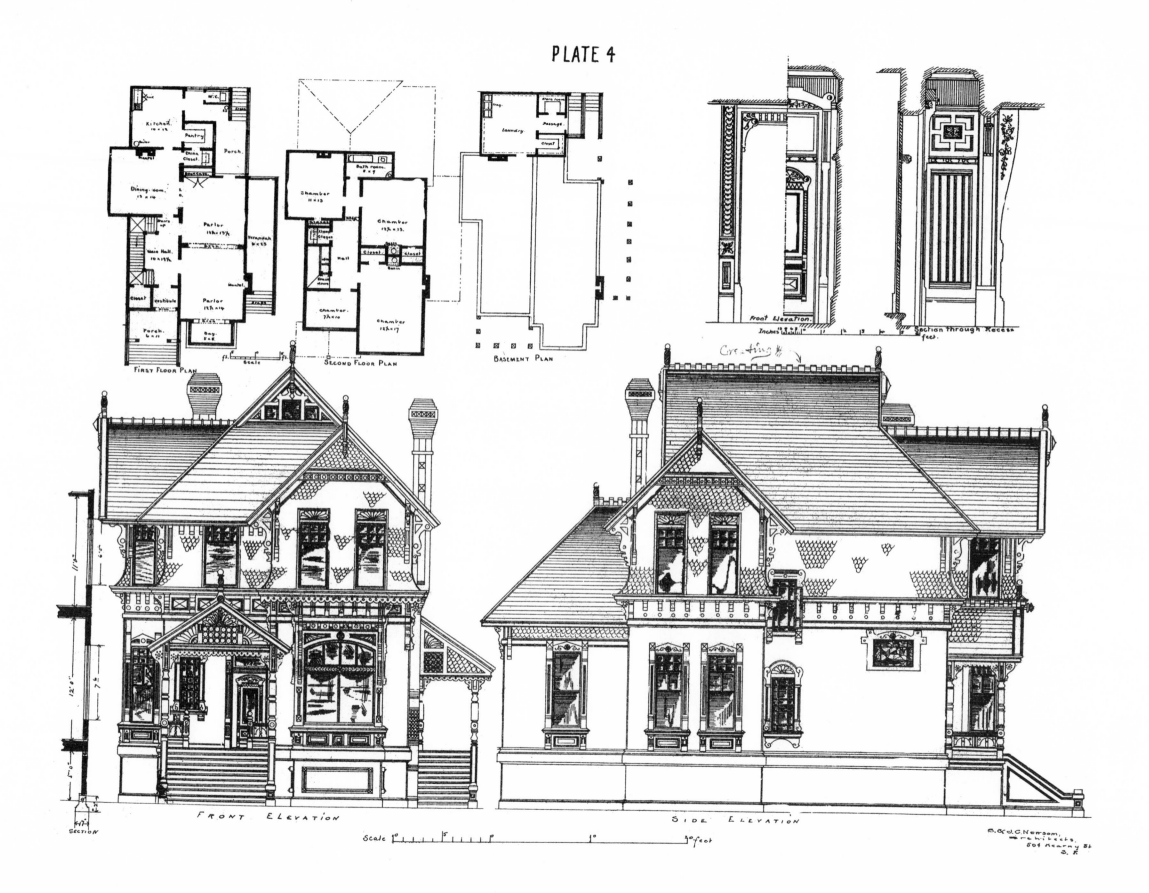

FIRST FLOOR PLAN

SECOND FLOOR PLAN

BASEMENT PLAN

Front Elevation.

Section Through Recess

FRONT ELEVATION

SIDE ELEVATION

SECTION

Scale

S. & J. C. Newsom,
Architects.
504 Kearny St.
S. F.

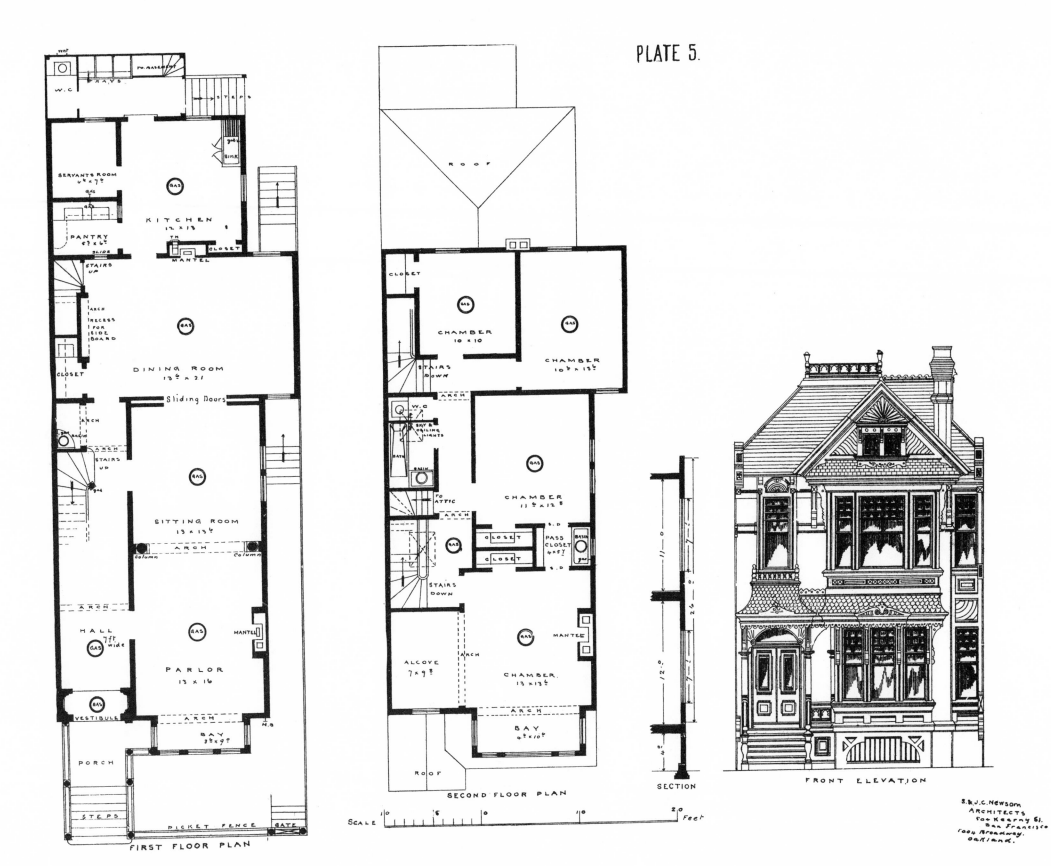

PLATE 5.

FIRST FLOOR PLAN

W.C.

TRAPS

TO BASEMENT

STEPS

SINK

SERVANTS ROOM
6⁴ x 7⁹

GAS

KITCHEN
12 x 13

GAS

PANTRY
6⁹ x 6⁴

SLIDE

CLOSET
MANTEL

STAIRS UP

ARCH

RECESS FOR SIDE BOARD

CLOSET

DINING ROOM
13⁴ x 21

GAS

Sliding Doors

ARCH

BASIN
ARCH
STAIRS UP

SITTING ROOM
13 x 13⁴

GAS

ARCH
Column   Column

HALL
7 ft. wide
GAS

MANTEL

PARLOR
13 x 16

GAS

ARCH

GAS
VESTIBULE

ARCH

N.B

BAY
3³ x 9°

PORCH

STEPS

PICKET FENCE   GATE

SECOND FLOOR PLAN

ROOF

CLOSET

GAS

CHAMBER
10 x 10

GAS

CHAMBER
10⁴ x 13⁴

STAIRS DOWN

ARCH

W.C.
SKY & CEILING LIGHTS
BATH
BASIN
TO ATTIC

ARCH

GAS

CHAMBER
11⁴ x 12⁸

CLOSET   PASS CLOSET
4 x 5⁷   BASIN
CLOSET

S.D.

GAS

S.D.

STAIRS DOWN

ARCH

ALCOVE
7 x 9⁸

MANTEL

CHAMBER
13 x 13⁴

GAS

ARCH

BAY
4⁴ x 10⁴

ROOF

SECTION

11'-0"
26'-0"
12'-0"
7'-1"
4'-0"
7'-1"

FRONT ELEVATION

S. & J.C. Newsom
ARCHITECTS
70½ Kearny St.
San Francisco
1004 Broadway,
Oakland.

SCALE 10   5   0   10   20 Feet

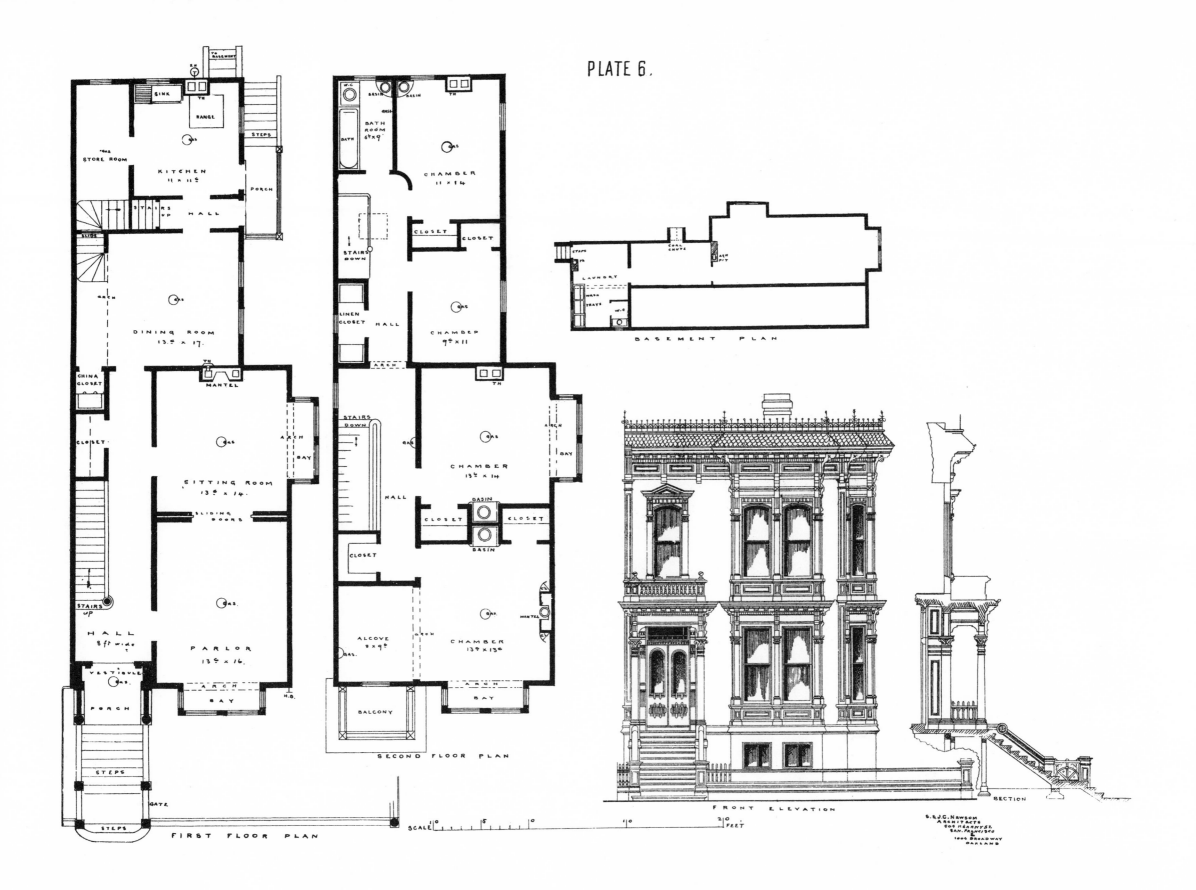

PLATE 6.

FIRST FLOOR PLAN

SECOND FLOOR PLAN

BASEMENT PLAN

FRONT ELEVATION

SECTION

SCALE

FEET

PLATE 7.

First Floor Plan:

Yard to be jet anked with rev bebelled & Dressed oregon on 3"x4" R.W. sleepers and 1'6"

To Cellur
Hopper & Hosebib
Porch
Down To Yard
Fire
Sink
Pantry 4'9"x5'6"
Passage

Servants Rm. 8'x8'
Sink
Kitchen 12'x13'6"
Closet. 5 drawers.
Boiler Th.
China Cl.
Mantels ash flue.
Sideboard Drawers under.

Dining Room. 13'6"x20'3"

Sliding Doors 9ft. 6 high x 13½ thick.

Hall. 7 ft. wide. 5'x16'
Clo.
Mantel & ash flue
Passage walk

Parlor. 13'x17'
Vestibule
Arched
Bay. 3'6"x8'6"
Arch.

Porch
Arched
Steps to Garden
Garden.
Gate
Steps to Sidewalk.
Walk rev bevelled & Dressed oregon

25'—0"

First Floor Plan.

Second Story Plan:

Ink
Bath Rm W.C.
Basin
Clo. 2'6"x6'6"
Chamber. 13'6"x13'0"

Closet
Hall
Arch
Hall
Skylight over.
Chamber. 13'6"x16'6"
Clo.
Basin
Clo.

Chamber. 7'x11'0"
Chamber. 13'x15'5"
Balcony.
Bay. 3'6"x8'
Arch.

Second Story Plan.

Detail of Stairs
Inches 12 9 6 3 0   1   2 feet.
Scale for Details.

Detail of Wainscotting.

Section
11'0"   26'0"   12'0"   7'1"   4'4"

Front Elevation.

Samuel and Jos. C. Newsom, Architects
504 Kearny Street, San Francisco

Scale. 10   5   0   10   20 feet.

PLATE 8.

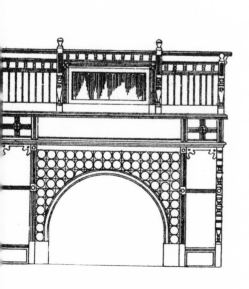

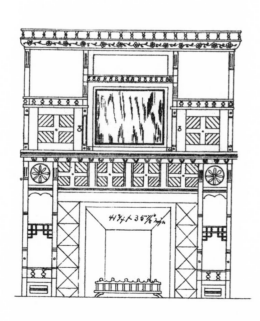

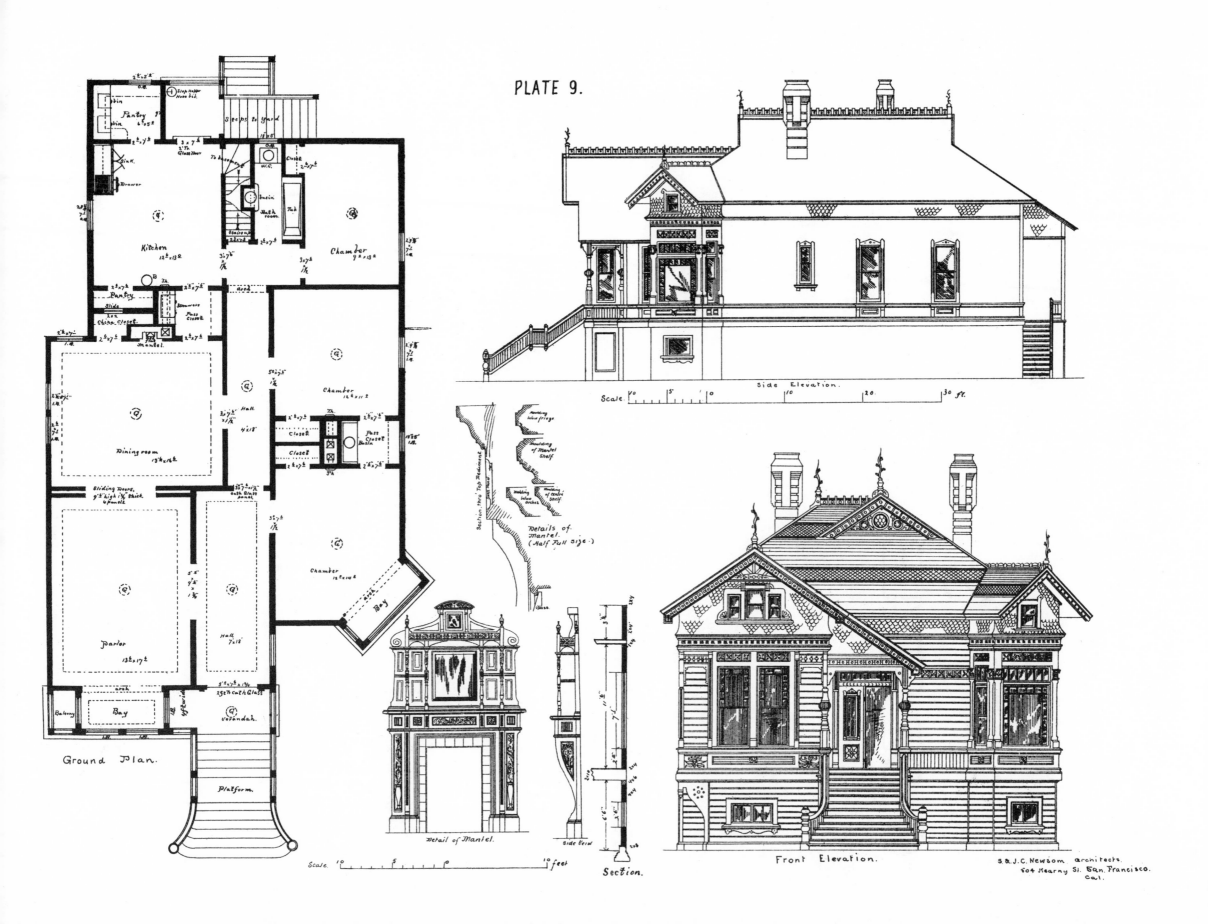

PLATE 9.

Side Elevation.

Scale

Details of Mantel.
(Half Full Size.)

Ground Plan.

Detail of Mantel.

Side View

Section.

Scale

Front Elevation.

S. & J. C. Newsom. Architects.
504 Kearny St. San Francisco.
Cal.

BLUM, EPPSTEIN & MARSH

MANUFACTURERS AND IMPORTERS OF

Parquet Flooring & Wood Carpeting

RICH AND PLAIN FURNITURE, WOODEN MANTELS, CARPETS AND INTERIOR DECORATIONS,

Office and Show Rooms: 126 Kearny Street, - - - Factory: 209 to 227 Fell Street,

SAN FRANCISCO.

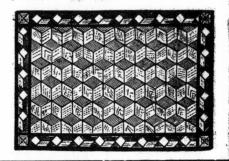

D. N. & C. A. HAWLEY

AGENTS

HOWE'S STANDARD SCALES

NEWTON FARM AND HEADER WAGONS,

Plows, Harrows and Cultivators,

AMESBURY & GOULD DAVIS PHAETONS, BUGGIES, ETC., ETC.

Crescent Coffee Mills, White's Money Drawers,

A FULL LINE OF BUILDERS' HARDWARE,

501 to 507 Market Street,

CORNER FIRST STREET. SAN FRANCISCO, CAL.

STAINED GLASS

For Domestic and Church uses, made up in the highest art by the LA FARGE DECORATIVE CO. of New York, the leading authority in the United States on Decorative Art.

MEMORIAL ÷ WINDOWS

A Specialty. Samples on exhibition at our store. Call and see them.

Glacier Decoration, or Imitation Stained Glass

The best manufactured in the world. Suitable for all purposes, and any one can apply it. A full stock of varied designs constantly on hand.

PICTURE MOULDINGS,

PLAIN AND TARRED SHEATHING PAPER, OR BUILDING BOARD,

WALL PAPERS,

American, French and English—Artistic Designs.

FRESCOING and all kinds of INTERIOR DECORATING done in an artistic manner by skilled artists.

Manufacturers of *Window Shades.* All kinds in stock or made to order. CORNICE POLES AND FITTINGS.

G. W. CLARK & CO.

645 & 647 Market Street.

Beautiful Tiles. Moderate

IN DESIGN. IN PRICE.

HEARTHS

Facings, Floorings & Wainscotings

A Large and Varied Stock of

GRATES, OPEN FIRE PLACES

Fenders, Andirons, etc.

The Largest and Finest Stock of

Lamps and Chandeliers

On the Pacific Coast.

THOMAS DAY & CO.

PLUMBING SUPPLIES A SPECIALTY.

122 & 124 SUTTER ST.

San Francisco.

AGENTS FOR AMERICAN METER CO'S GAS STOVES AND RANGES.

NEW DESIGNS! NOTHING COMMON!

FIRST-CLASS WORK AT LOWEST PRICES.

PHENIX IRON WORKS

18 & 20 FREMONT ST., SAN FRANCISCO.

It is to the interest of Architects, Contractors and Builders to examine our designs and prices before purchasing inferior goods of other manufacture. Catalogues to be had upon application.

WROUGHT AND MALLEABLE IRON

Fencing and House Crestings

Colored, Enameled and Photographic Glass, and German Looking Glass Plates,

◀ FRENCH ⚬ PLATE ⚬ GLASS ▶

Fr. H. ROSENBAUM & CO.

Importers of French, German and English

Window Glass and Crystal Sheet.

Manufacturers of Mirror Plates and Frames,

567 Market Street,

Opposite Sansome Street. SAN FRANCISCO.

DYCKERHOFF PORTLAND CEMENT

Of Unrivalled Strength, Fineness and Reliability,

IS THE BEST AND CHEAPEST FOR FOUNDATIONS, CELLARS, FLOORS, WALKS, ARTIFICIAL STONE, ETC.

These extraordinary qualities permit an unusually large addition of sand, etc. (25 to 50 per cent. more than other well-known Portland Cements), and will produce the strongest, most reliable and durable work.

Selling at no higher figure than ordinary good brands of Portland Cement, it is therefore much the cheapest to use.

Dyckerhoff's Portland Cement is always uniform, unalterable in volume, and will not crack.

The packages (each barrel weighs 400 lbs. gross) are always in excellent condition and will bear handling and transportation without loss. Pamphlet containing directions and testimonials sent free.

CHAS. DUISENBERG & CO., 314 Sacramento St., San Francisco, Cal., Sole Agents for the Pacific Coast.

W. D. PERINE
MANUFACTURER OF
ARTIFICIAL STONE SIDEWALKS,

Garden Walks, Basement Floors, Carriage Steps, Colored Tiles, Building Stone, Urns, Vases, Stone Coping and Steps, Entrance to Cemetery Lots, Caskets, Stone Fountain Basins, etc.

San Francisco Office, 22 New Montgomery St. Oakland Office, 457 Ninth St.
Residence, 809 Oak St., Oakland.

TURNER, KENNEDY & SHAW

Lumber Dealers,

FOURTH AND CHANNEL STS., SAN FRANCISCO.

Yard connects direct with the C. P. and S. P. R. R., also with the Shipping.

JULIUS FINCK.   SIM BLUM.

WILL & FINCK

Importing and Manufacturing

CUTLERS,

LOCKSMITHS

—— AND ——

BELL HANGERS,

Barber Goods,
Sporting Goods,
Bar Goods
AND
Police Goods.

769 MARKET STREET, - - - - SAN FRANCISCO.

A. BERSON & SON

IMPORTERS AND DEALERS IN

CARPETS, OIL CLOTHS, ART DRAPERY

AND UPHOLSTERING GOODS,

26 Post Street, below Kearny, College Building, - San Francisco

Plain and Decorative Painting, Frescoing and Paper Hanging.

C. A. HOOPER.   TELEPHONE No. 5244.   G. W. HOOPER.

A. M. JEWELL & CO.

South Point Mills,

BERRY STREET,

Bet. Third and Fourth,   San Francisco.

Planing and Sawing of all Descriptions.

Manufacturers of Wooden Tanks, Mouldings, Sash, Blinds, Doors, Frames, Shutters and Woodwork of every description.

Also, Manufacturers of

WOODEN PUMPS AND PIPE.

THOMAS MORTON'S SASH CHAINS,

For Suspending Wood Sashes, Doors, Gates, etc.   Strength from 25 lbs. to 2,000 lbs

FRANK P. LATSON & CO.

Wholesale and Retail Dealers in

HARDWARE

FINEST BRONZE GOODS A SPECIALTY.

BUILDERS' MATERIALS, BURGLAR-PROOF LOCKS, CARPENTERS' TOOLS.

Agents for LOUDERBACK'S PERFECT WINDOW SCREEN

These Screens are unrivalled for beauty, convenience and cheapness.   There is no carpenter work to do; any one can fit them properly.   Price Lists forwarded on application.

F. P. LATSON & CO., 28 NEW MONTGOMERY STREET, UNDER PALACE HOTEL, SAN FRANCISCO

CARGOES SAWED TO ORDER

SPARS AND PILES

CONSTANTLY ON HAND.

HANSON & CO.
Lumber Dealers
AND MANUFACTURERS OF
PINE & REDWOOD LUMBER

Mill at Tacoma, W. T.   Branch House, Redwood City.

OFFICE AND YARD

Pier 11, Steuart Street, San Francisco

PLATE 10

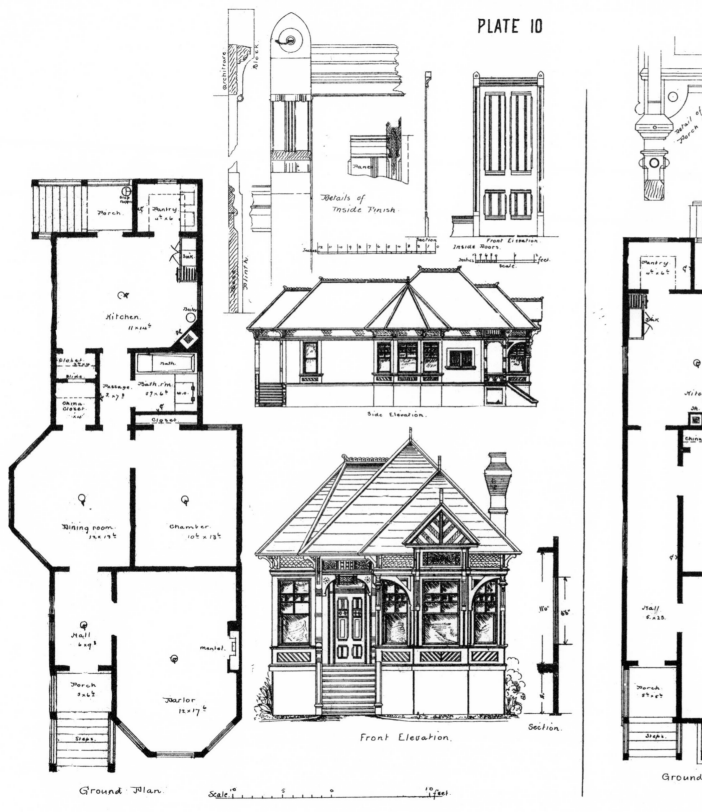

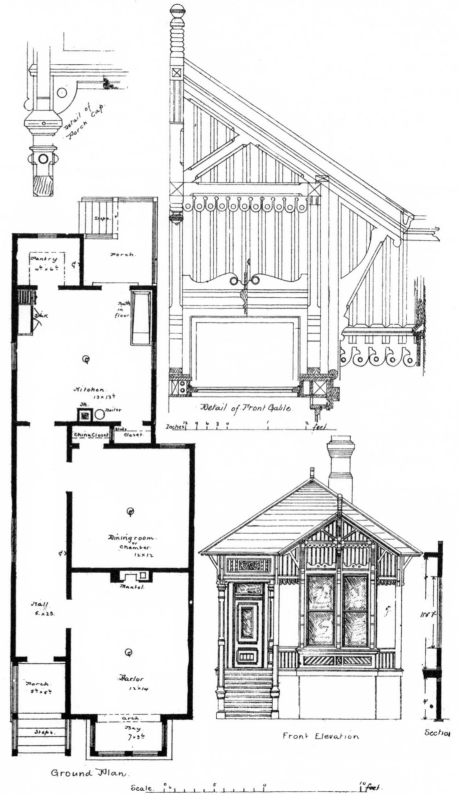

Details of Inside Finish.

Front Elevation. Inside Doors.

Detail of Porch Cap.

Side Elevation.

Detail of Front Gable.

Front Elevation.

Section.

Ground Plan.

Scale. 5 0 10 feet

S. & J. C. Newsom. Architects.
504 Kearny St.
San Francisco. Cal.

PLATE II.

Second Floor Plan.

Chamber 14⁴ x 17⁴

Hall 6 x 22

Closet

Stairs up

Stairs down

Well

Bath

Bathroom 3 x 6

Chamber 12 x 12⁴

Arch

Alcove 4 x 8

Closet

Closet

Dressing room 7 x 8

Closet

Chamber 10⁴ x 15⁴

Chamber 15⁴ x 17

First Floor Plan.

Parlor 14⁴ x 17⁴

Mantel

Mantel

Main Hall 10 x 17⁴

Arch

Closet

Arch

Verandah 14 x 21

Steps

Arch

Library 13 x 16

Closet

Stairs down

Stairs up

Butlers Pantry 7⁴ x 11

Stairs up

Hall 6 x 7⁴

Arch

Arch

Dining room 17⁴ x 17⁴

Mantel

Mantel

Dumb Waiter

Pantry 6⁴ x 10

Scale

Basement Plan.

Cellar 14 x 17

Laundry 11 x 13⁴

Hall 7 x 13⁴

Passage

Stairs up

Kitchen 14⁴ x 17

Dumb waiter

Pantry 6 x 9⁴

Furnace room 13 x 15

Scale

Side Elevation.

Front Elevation.

S. & J. C. Newsom, Architects. 504 Kearny St. San Francisco.

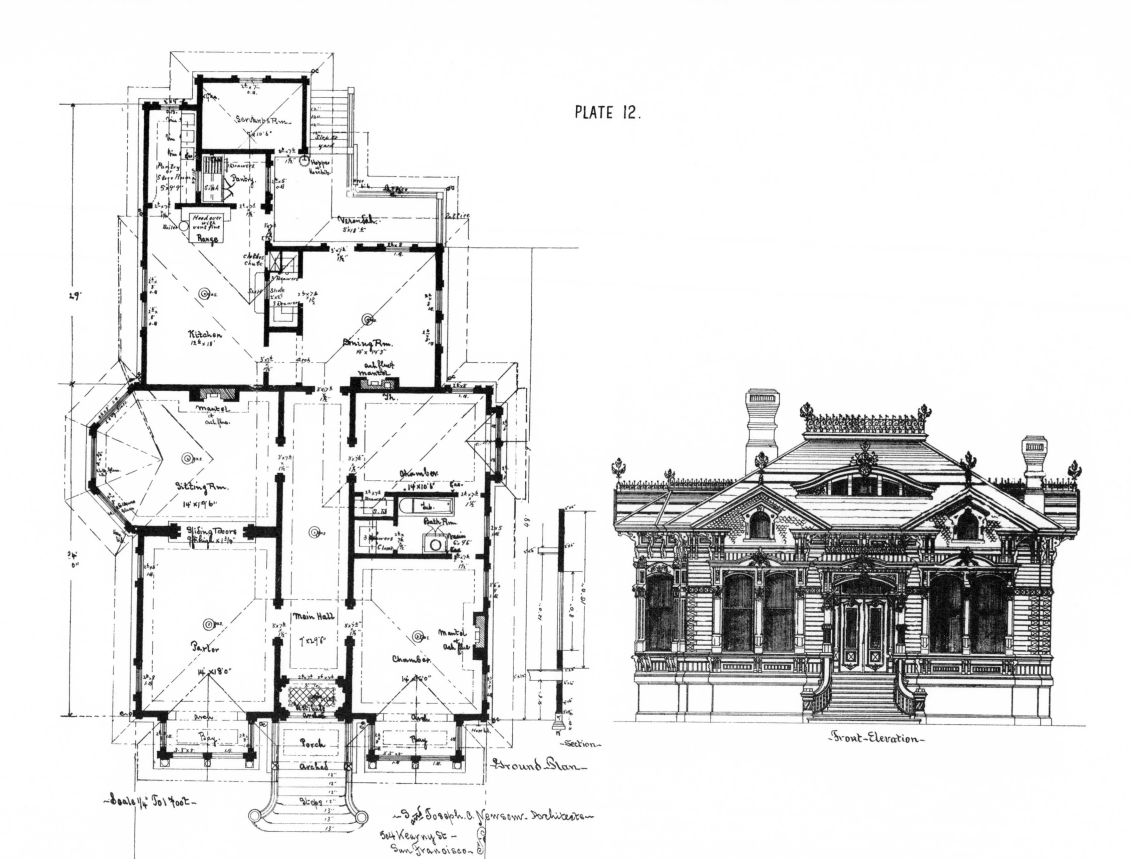

PLATE 12.

Front-Elevation-

Ground-Plan-

~Section~

~Scale ¼" to 1 foot~

~Samⁿᵈ Joseph C. Newsom Architects~
504 Kearny St
San Francisco

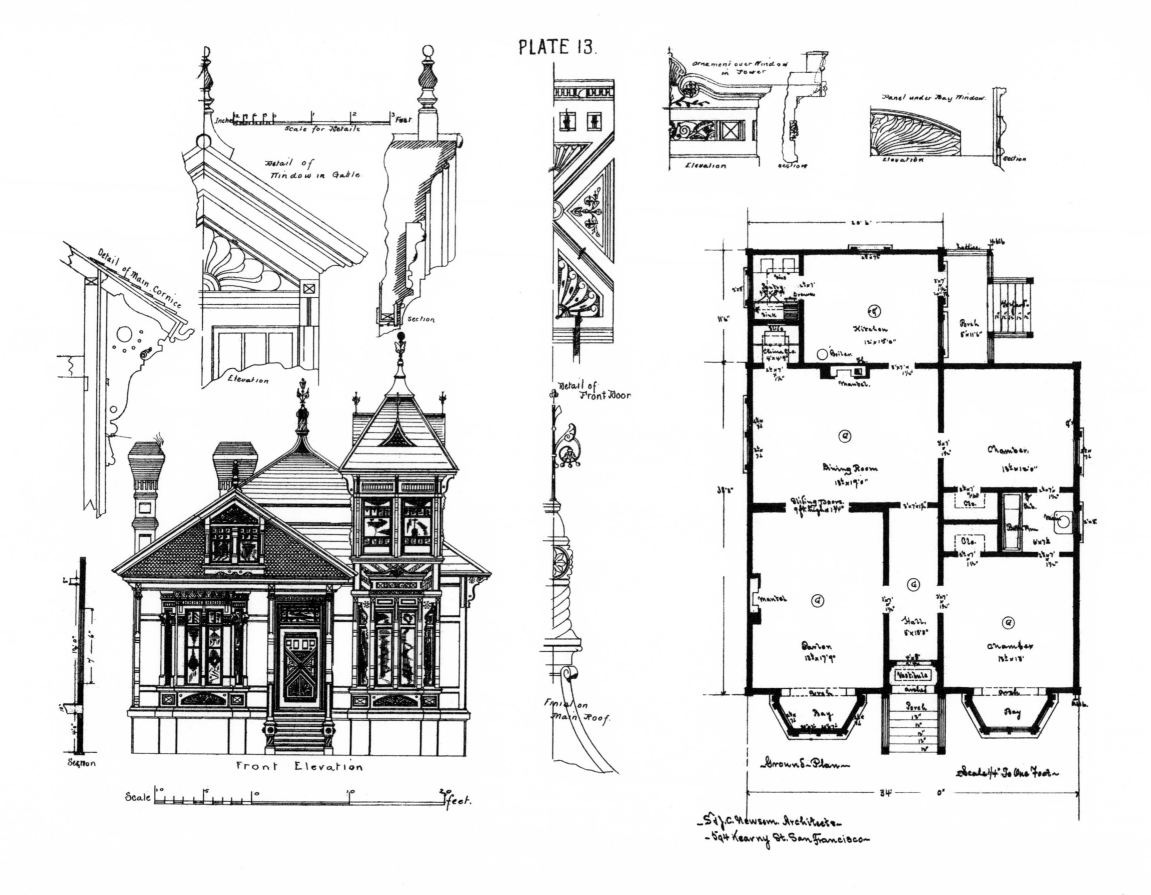

PLATE 13.

Scale for Details

Detail of Window in Gable

Detail of Main Cornice

Elevation

Section

Section

ornament over Window in Tower

Elevation   section

Panel under Bay Window

Elevation   Section

Detail of Front Door

Finial on Main Roof

Section

Front Elevation

Scale   feet.

Ground Plan   Scale 1/4" To One Foot

Kitchen
12'x15'0"

Porch
5'x11'6"

Dining Room
13'x19'0"

Chamber
13'x16'10"

Sliding Doors
9ft high & 7'4"

Parlor
13'x17'9"

Hall
5'x18'3"

Chamber
13'x18'

Vestibule arched

Bay   Porch   Bay

Mantel

Mantel

S & J C Newsom Architects
594 Kearny St. San Francisco

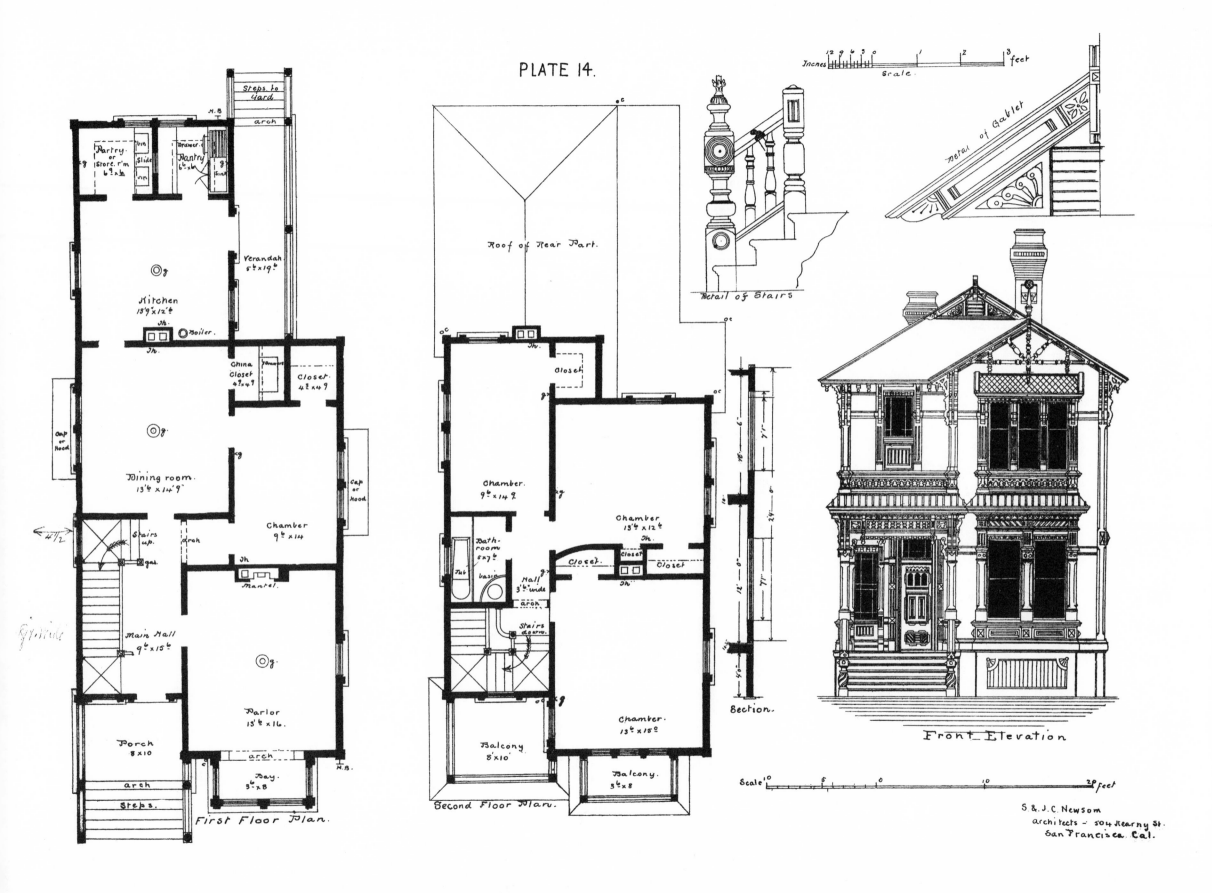

PLATE 14.

Scale.

Detail of Gablet

Detail of Stairs

Roof of Rear Part.

First Floor Plan.

Steps to Yard
arch
Pantry or Store rm
Pantry
Slide
Sink
Drawer
Sink
Verandah 5'x19'6"
Kitchen 18'9"x12'6"
Boiler.
China Closet 4'6"x4'9"
Closet 4'6"x4'9"
Cap or Hood
Dining room 13'6"x14'9"
Cap or Hood
Chamber 9'6"x14'
Stairs up.
arch
Mantel.
Main Hall 9'6"x15'6"
gas.
Parlor 13'6"x16'.
Porch 8'x10'
arch
Bay 3'6"x8'
arch
Steps

Second Floor Plan.

Closet
Chamber 9'6"x14'9"
Bathroom 5'x7'6"
Tub
basin
Chamber 13'6"x12'6"
Closet
Closet
Closet
Hall 3'6" wide
arch
Stairs down.
Balcony 8'x10'
Chamber 13'6"x15'2"
Balcony 5'6"x8'

Section.

Front Elevation.

Scale

S & J C Newsom
architects - 504 Kearny St.
San Francisco, Cal.

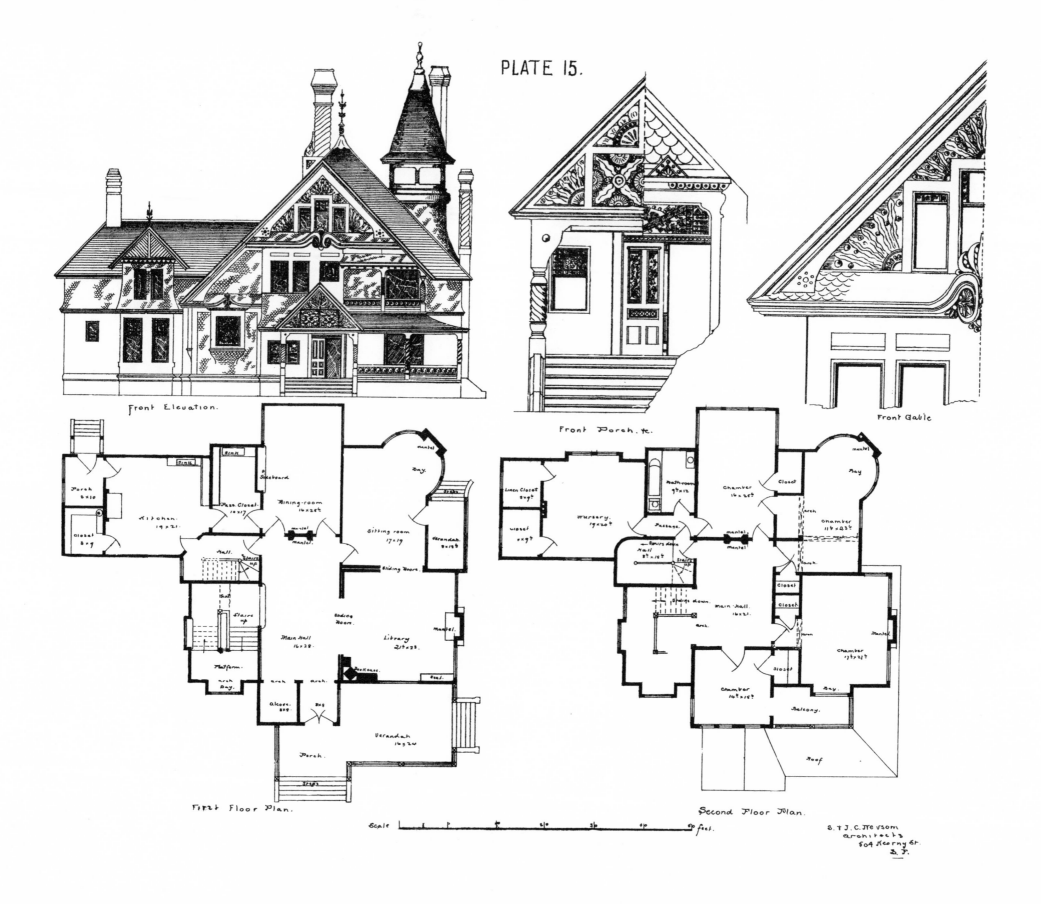

PLATE 15.

Front Elevation.

Front Porch. &c.

Front Gable

First Floor Plan.

Second Floor Plan.

Scale |___|___|___|___|___|___|___| feet.

S. & J. C. Newsom
architects
504 Kearny St.
S. F.

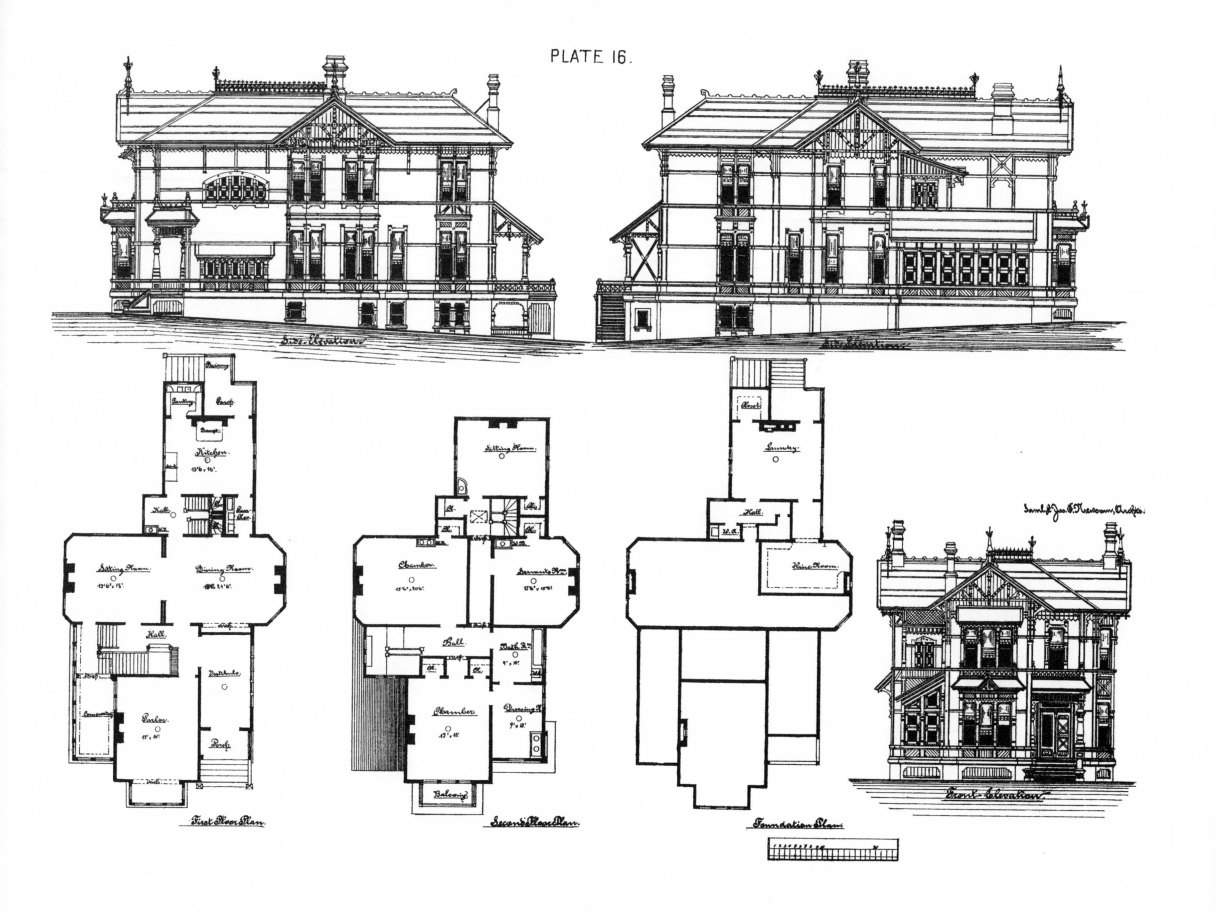

PLATE 16.

Side Elevation.

Side Elevation.

Saml. & Jas. C. Newsom, Archts.

First Floor Plan.

Second Floor Plan.

Foundation Plan.

Front Elevation.

PLATE 17.

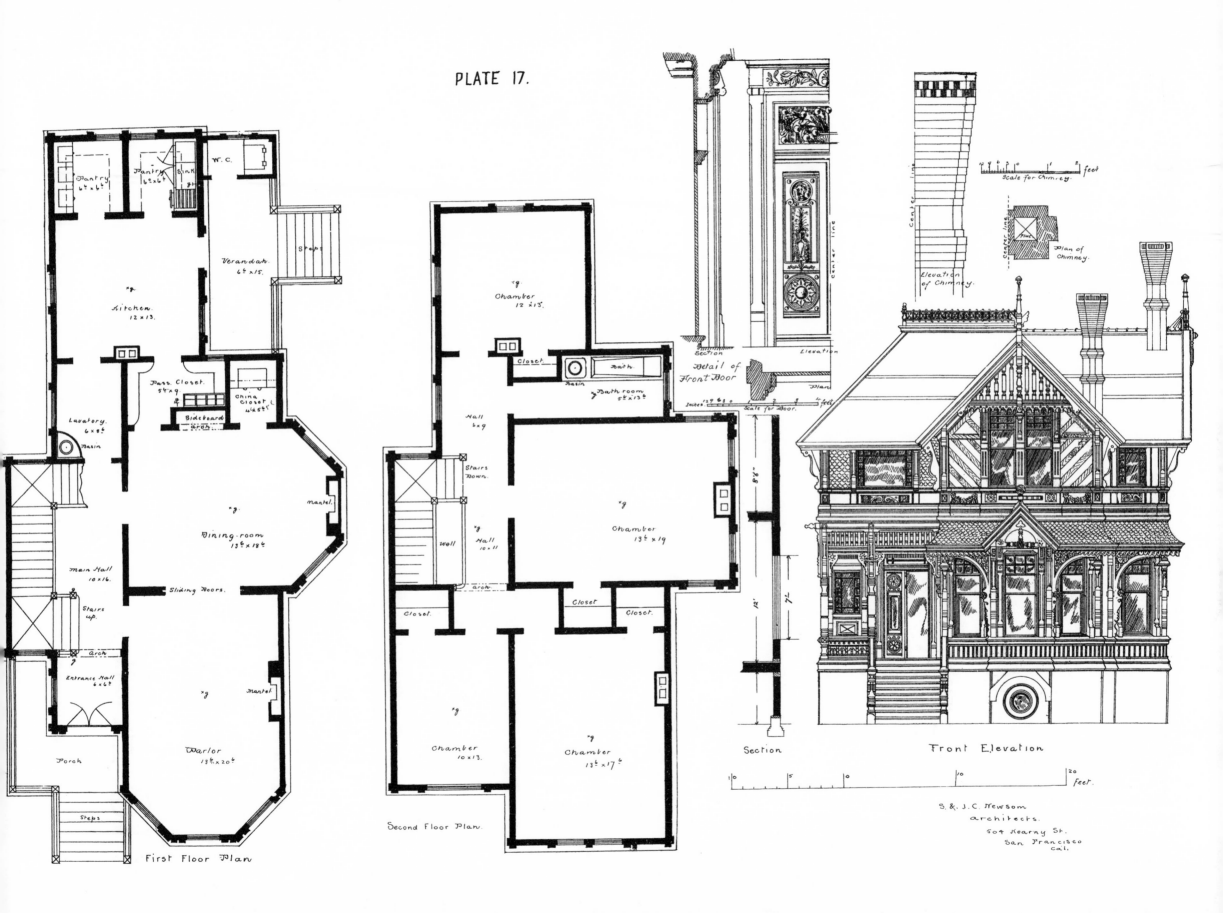

Pantry
6½ × 6½

Pantry
6½ × 6½

Sink

W. C.

Verandah.
6½ × 15.

Steps

*g
Kitchen.
12 × 13.

Pass. Closet.
5½ × 9

China
Closet 4½×5½

Sideboard
arch

Lavatory.
6 × 8½

Basin

*g
Dining-room
13½ × 18½

mantel.

Main Hall
10 × 16.

Sliding Doors.

Stairs
up.

Arch

Entrance Hall
6 × 6½

*g

mantel.

Porch

Parlor
13½×20½

Steps

First Floor Plan

*g
Chamber
12 × 15.

Closet

Basin

Bath

*g
Bath room
5½×13½

Hall
6 × 9

Stairs
Down.

Well

*g
Hall
10 × 11

*g
Chamber
13½ × 19

Closet

Closet

Closet

Closet.

*g
Chamber
10 × 13.

*g
Chamber
13½×17½

Second Floor Plan.

Section
Elevation

Detail of
Front Door

Inches 12 9 6 3 0   1   2   3   4 feet
Scale for Door.

8'8"

12'

7'½

Section

Center line

Flue

Plan of
Chimney.

Center line

Center line

Elevation
of Chimney.

9 6 3 0   1   2 feet
Scale for Chimney.

Front Elevation

10   5   10   10   20
feet

S. & J. C. Newsom
Architects.
504 Kearny St.
San Francisco
Cal.

PLATE 18.

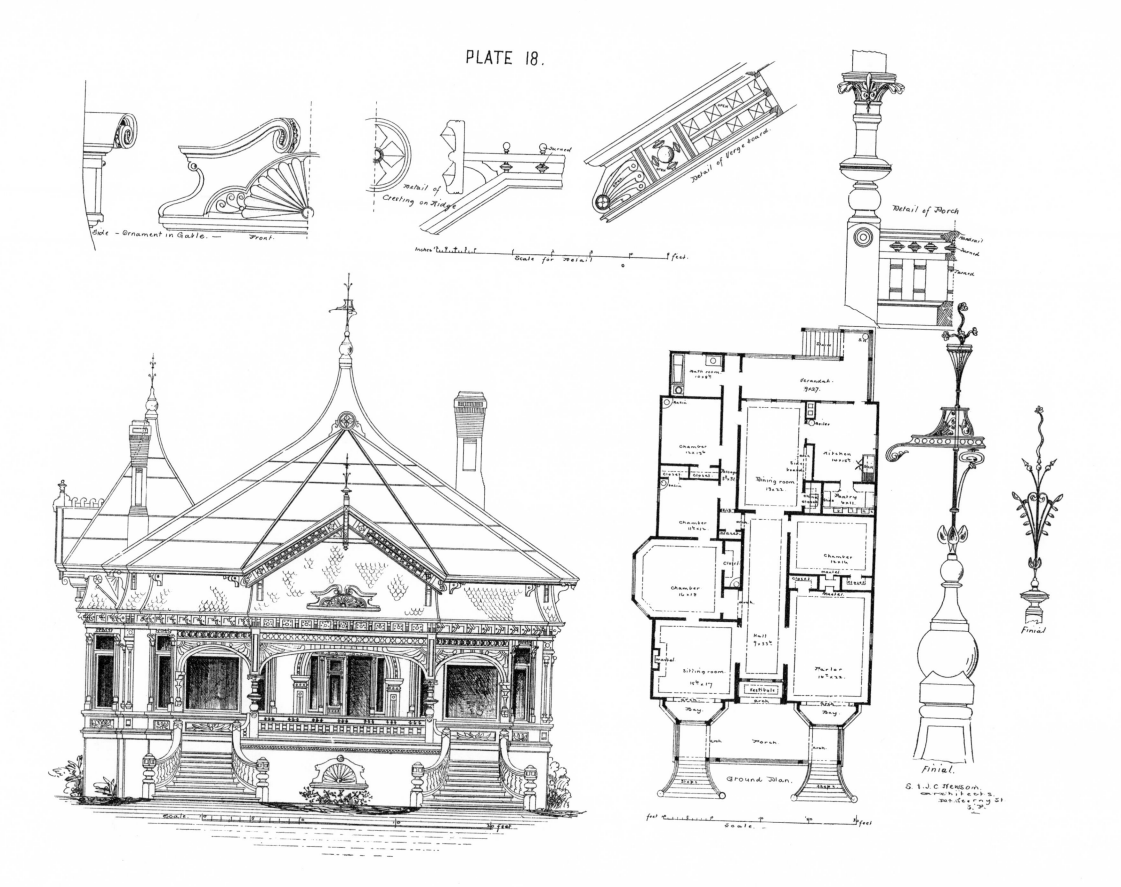

Side — Ornament in Gable. — Front.

Detail of Cresting on Ridge.

Detail of Verge Board.

Inches. Scale for Detail. 1 feet.

Detail of Porch

Ground Plan.

Bath room 10x8½

Verandah. 9x27.

Chamber 12x13½

Kitchen 14x16½

Dining room 15x22.

Pantry

Closet   Closet

Chamber 11½x14

Chamber 12x14

Chamber 16x19

Closet

Hall 9x33½

Parlor 14½x22.

Sitting room 15½x17

Vestibule Arch

Porch

Bay.   Bay.

Steps.   Steps.

feet. Scale.

S. & J.C. Newsom. architects. 325 Kearny St. S. F.

Finial.

Finial

PLATE 19.

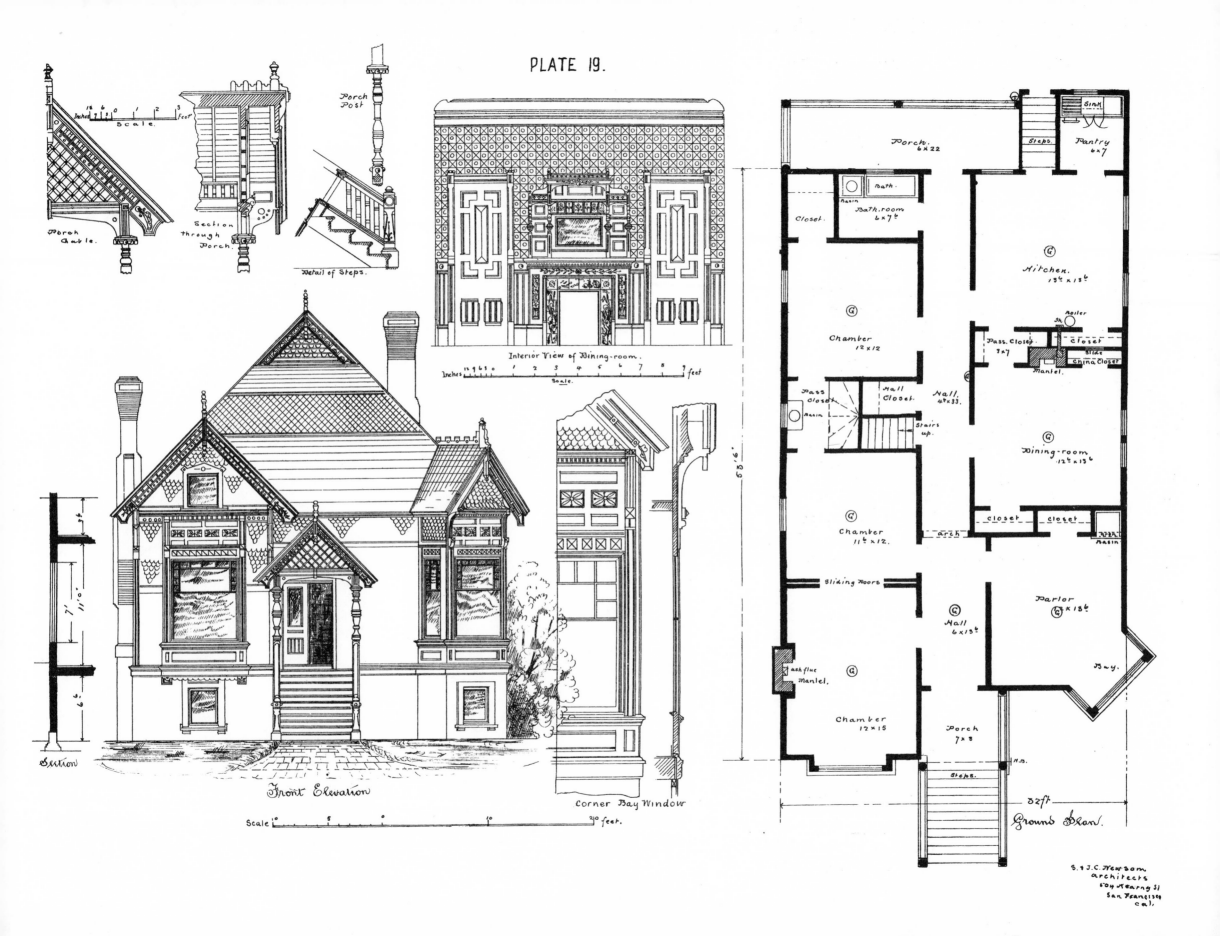

Scale.

Porch Post

Porch Gable.

Section through Porch.

Detail of Steps.

Interior View of Dining-room.

Inches 1 2 9 6 5 0   1   2   3   4   5   6   7   8   9 feet
Scale.

Section

Front Elevation

Scale   5   10   20 feet

Corner Bay Window

Ground Plan.

Porch. 6 x 22

Steps

Sink

Pantry 6 x 7

Closet

Bath

Bath-room 6 x 7½

Kitchen 13½ x 13½

Chamber 12 x 12

Boiler

Pass. Closet 3 x 7

Closet

Slide

China Closet

Mantel

Pass Closet

Hall Closet

Hall 4 x 33.

Stairs up.

Dining-room 12½ x 13½

Chamber 11½ x 12.

arch

closet

closet

Basin

Sliding Doors

Hall 6 x 13½

Parlor 13½ x 13½

Chamber 12 x 15

ash flue Mantel.

Bay.

Porch 7 x 8

Steps.

32 ft

S. & J.C. Newsom
Architects
504 Kearny St
San Francisco
Cal.

PLATE 20.

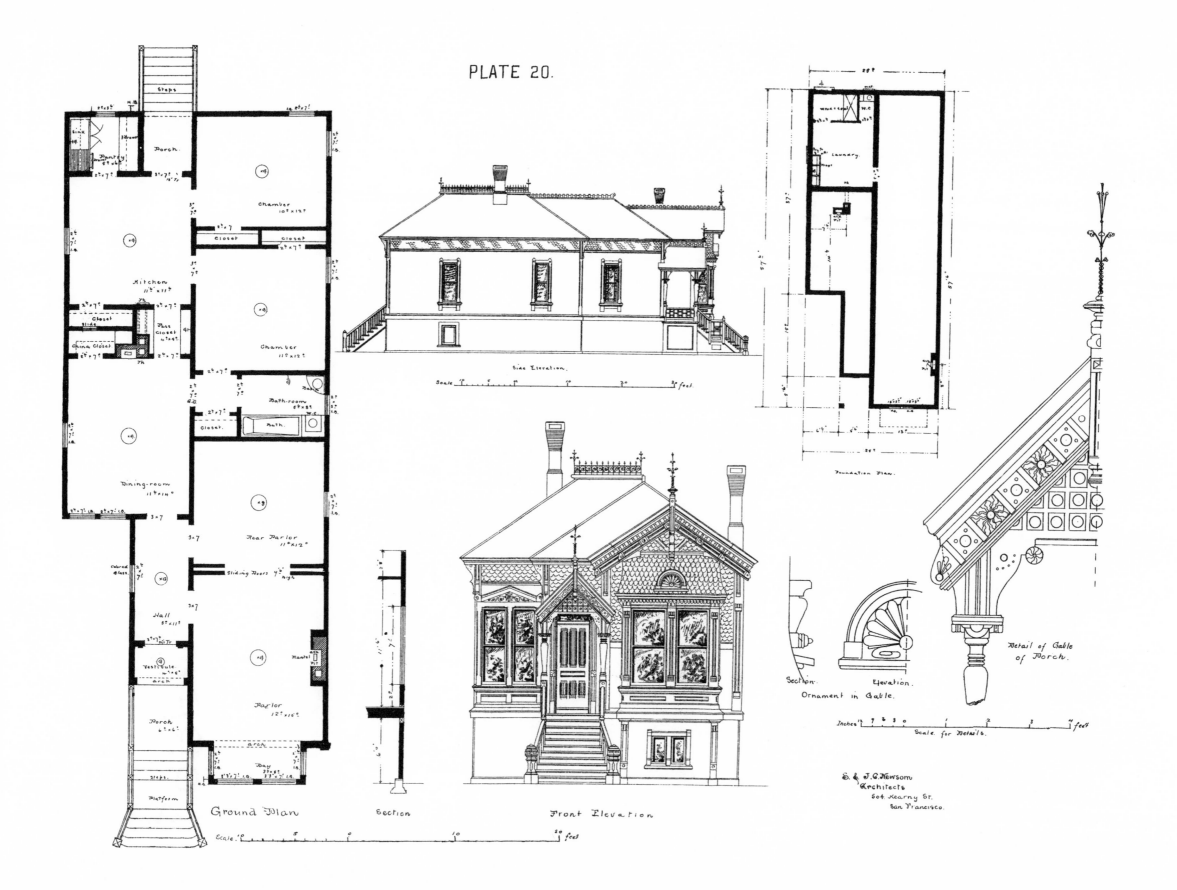

Ground Plan

Section

Front Elevation

Side Elevation.

Foundation Plan.

Detail of Gable
of Porch.

Section. Elevation.
Ornament in Gable.

S. & J. C. Newsom
Architects
604 Kearny St.
San Francisco.

PLATE 21

FIRST FLOOR PLAN

Porch. 7x28
pump waiter
cl.
Library. 13x14
Dining Rm. 14x18½
Bay 4x12
c.w.
cl.
Stairs down
Stairs up
Hall 9ft.
Parlor. 14x17½
Porch.
Bay.
1st Floor.

SECOND FLOOR PLAN

Chamber 13x13½
Harbour. 12x16½
Bay
Hall 12x13
Stairs down
Closet Closet
bath room &c. &c.
Closet
Chamber 9x10½
Chamber 14x14
Balcony.

BASEMENT PLAN

W.C.
Porch 7x18
Pantry 5x7
Servants room. 9x9
Dumb waiter
Store room 5x9
Range
Kitchen 13x17½
Hall 11½x13
Stairs up

Scale for Plans.

FRONT ELEVATION

SECTION.

SIDE ELEVATION

Scale for Elevations.

G. & J. C. Newsom
architects
504 Kearny St.
S.F.

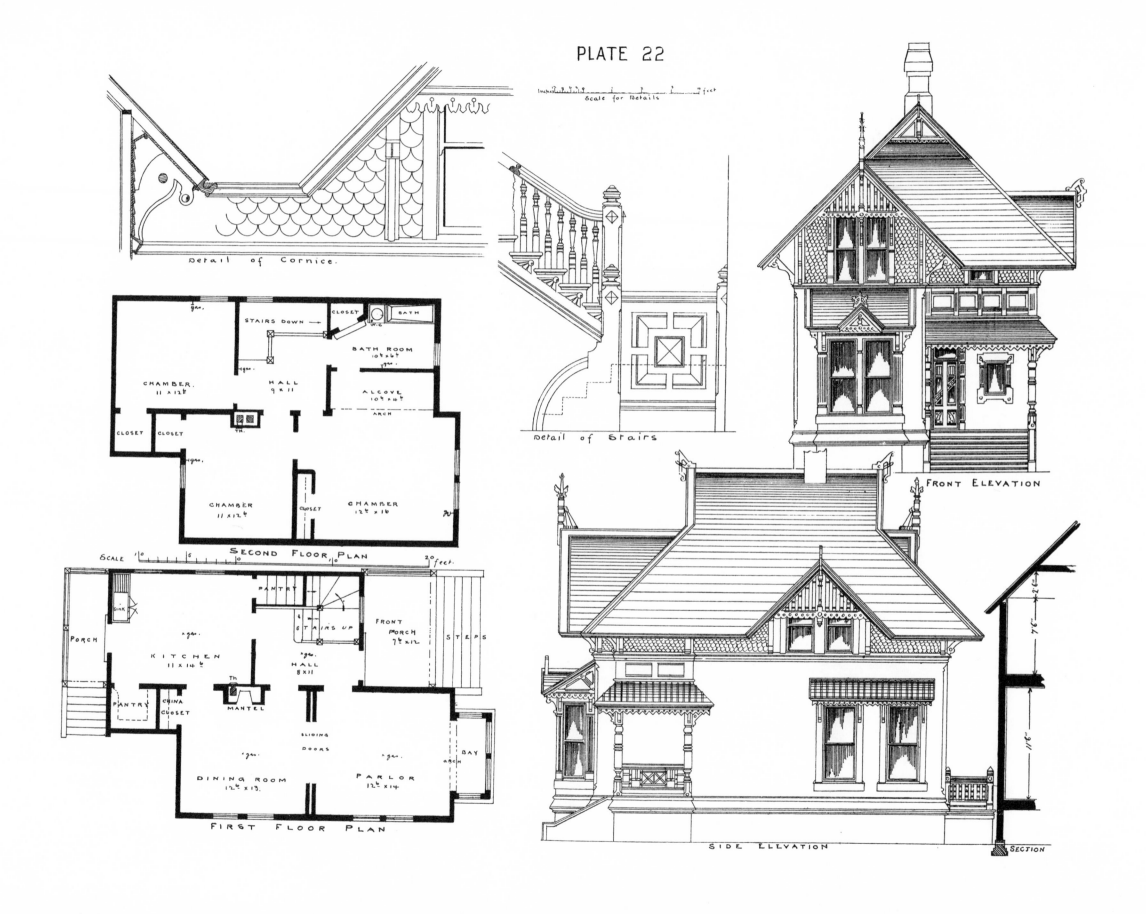

PLATE 22

Detail of Cornice.

Scale for Details

Detail of Stairs

Front Elevation

SECOND FLOOR PLAN

CHAMBER.
11 x 12½

HALL
9 x 11

STAIRS DOWN →

CLOSET

BATH

BATH ROOM
10½ x 6½

ALCOVE
10½ x 14½

ARCH

CLOSET CLOSET

CHAMBER
11 x 12½

CLOSET

CHAMBER
12½ x 16

Scale

FIRST FLOOR PLAN

PORCH

SINK

PANTRY

STAIRS UP

FRONT PORCH
7½ x 12

STEPS

KITCHEN
11 x 14½

HALL
8 x 11

PANTRY

CHINA CLOSET

MANTEL

SLIDING DOORS

DINING ROOM
12½ x 13

PARLOR
12½ x 14

BAY

ARCH

SIDE ELEVATION

SECTION

PLATE 23

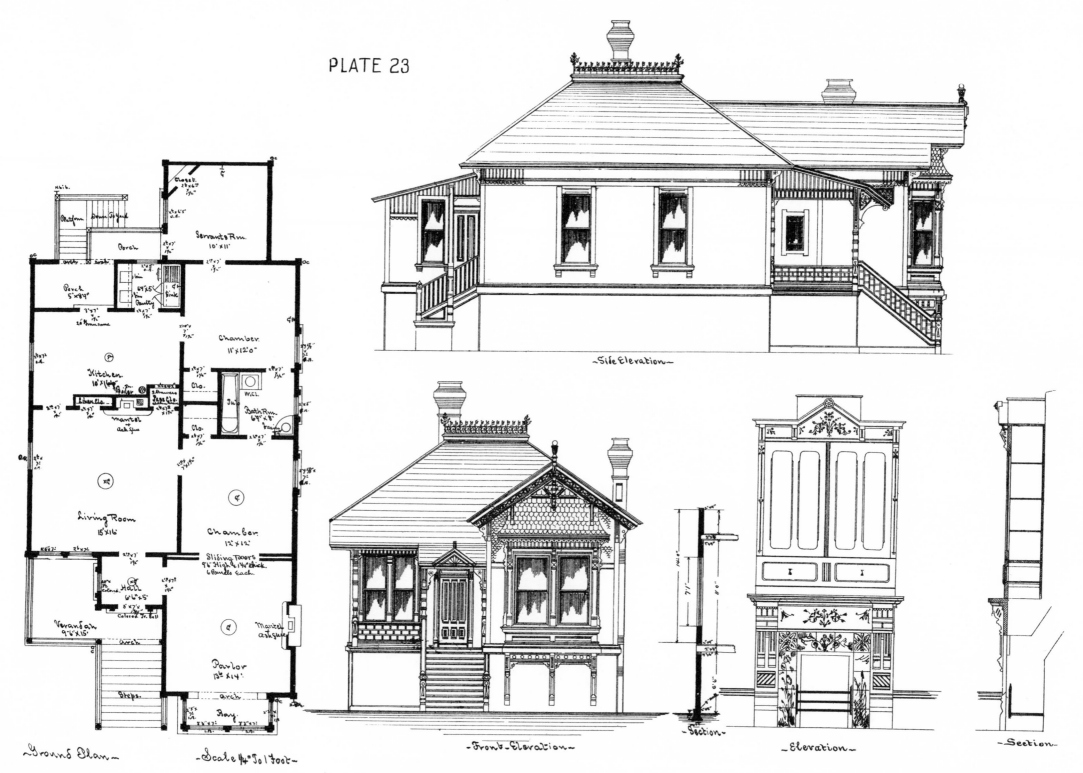

— Side Elevation —

— Ground Plan —   — Scale ¼″ To 1 foot —

— Front Elevation —   — Section —   — Elevation —   — Section —

Samuel and Jos. C. Newsom, Architects &c.
504 Kearny Street — 1004 Broadway
San Francisco — Oakland —

— Scale 1 Inch To 1 foot —

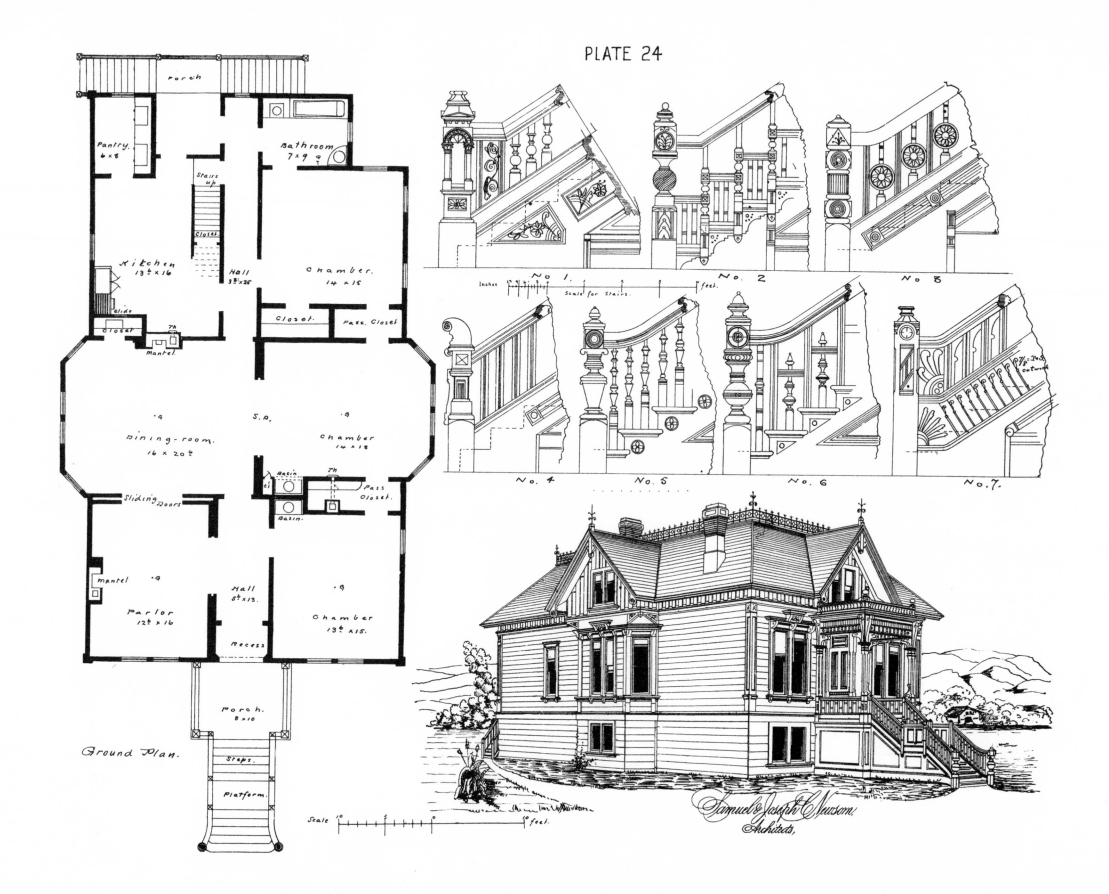

PLATE 24

No 1. No. 2. No 3.

Inches | | Scale for Stairs. | feet.

No. 4. No. 5. No. 6. No.7.

Porch

Pantry.
6 x 8

Bathroom
7 x 9

Kitchen
13½ x 16

Stairs
up

Closet

Hall
3½ x 25

Chamber.
14 x 15

Slide

Closet

7h
Closet

mantel.

Closet.

Pass. Closet

S.P.

Dining-room.
16 x 20½

Chamber
14 x 15

Basin

7h

Pass
Closet.

Sliding Doors

Basin.

mantel

Hall
5½ x 13.

Parlor
12½ x 16

Chamber
13½ x 15.

Recess

Ground Plan.

Porch.
8 x 10

Steps.

Platform.

Scale | | | | feet.

Samuel & Joseph C. Newsom,
Architects,

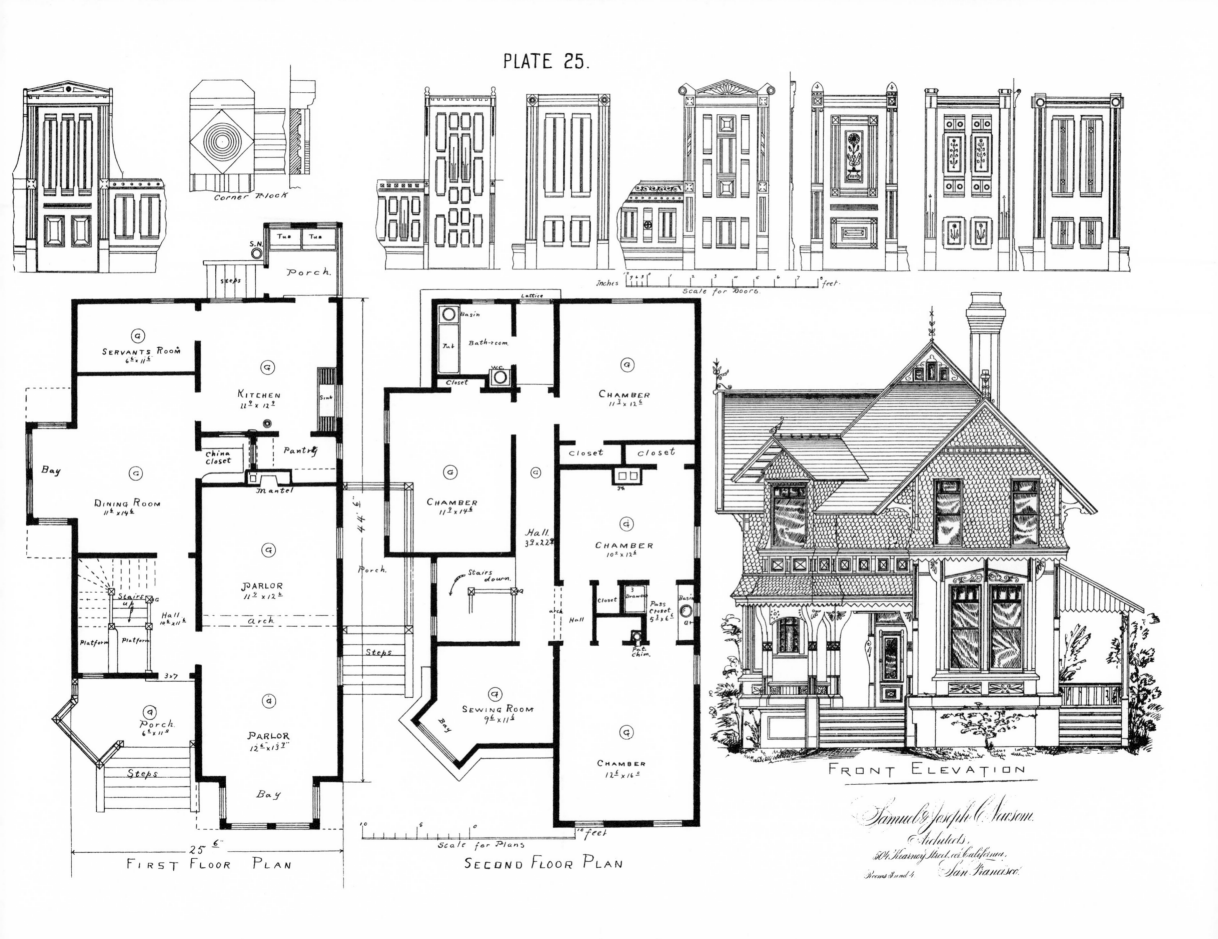

PLATE 25.

Corner Block

Inches | Scale for Doors | feet.

FIRST FLOOR PLAN

Servants Room 6ᵉ x 11ᵉ

Porch.

Kitchen 11ᵉ x 12ᵉ

Sink

Pantry

China Closet

Mantel

Bay

Dining Room 11ᵉ x 14ᵉ

Stairs up

Hall 10ᵉ x 11ᵉ

Parlor 11ᵉ x 12ᵉ

Platform

Platform

arch.

3 x 7

44' 6"

Porch.

Steps

Parlor 12ᵉ x 13ᵉ

Porch. 6ᵉ x 11ᵉ

Steps

Bay

25 6"

SECOND FLOOR PLAN

Lattice

Basin

Tub

Bath-room.

W.C.

Closet

Chamber 11ᵉ x 12ᵉ

Closet | Closet

Chamber 11ᵉ x 14ᵉ

Hall 39 x 22ᵉ

Stairs down.

Chamber 10ᵉ x 12ᵉ

Closet

3 Drawer

Pass Closet 5ᵉ x 6ᵉ

Basin

Pat. Chim.

Sewing Room 9ᵉ x 11ᵉ

Bay

Chamber 12ᵉ x 16ᵉ

Scale for Plans | feet

FRONT ELEVATION

Samuel & Joseph C. Newsom.
Architects,
504 Kearney Street, cor. California,
San Francisco.
Rooms 3 and 4

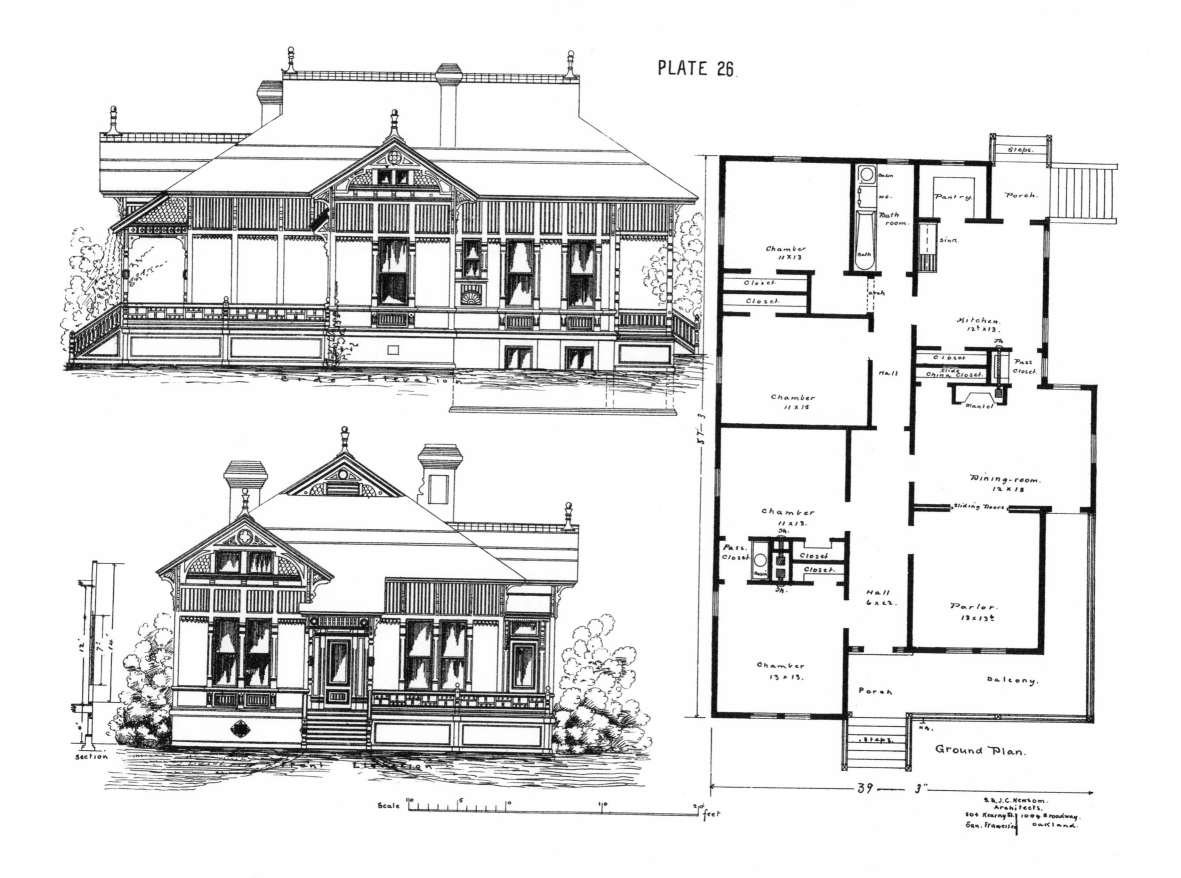

PLATE 26.

Side Elevation

Front Elevation

Ground Plan.

Chamber
11 x 13

Closet
Closet

Hall

Chamber
11 x 13

Chamber
11 x 13.

Pass.
Closet

Closet
Closet

Hall
6 x 22.

Chamber
13 x 13.

Porch

Steps.

Steps.

Bath
room.

Basin

w.c.

Bath

sink

Pantry.

Porch

Kitchen.
12½ x 13.

Closet
China Closet.
Slide

Pass
Closet

Mantel

Dining-room.
12 x 18

Sliding Doors

Parlor.
13 x 13½

Balcony.

37' - 3"

39 — 3"

Scale   5   0   10   20 feet

section

S. & J. C. Newsom.
Architects.
504 Kearny St. 1004 Broadway.
San Francisco Oakland.

PLATE 27

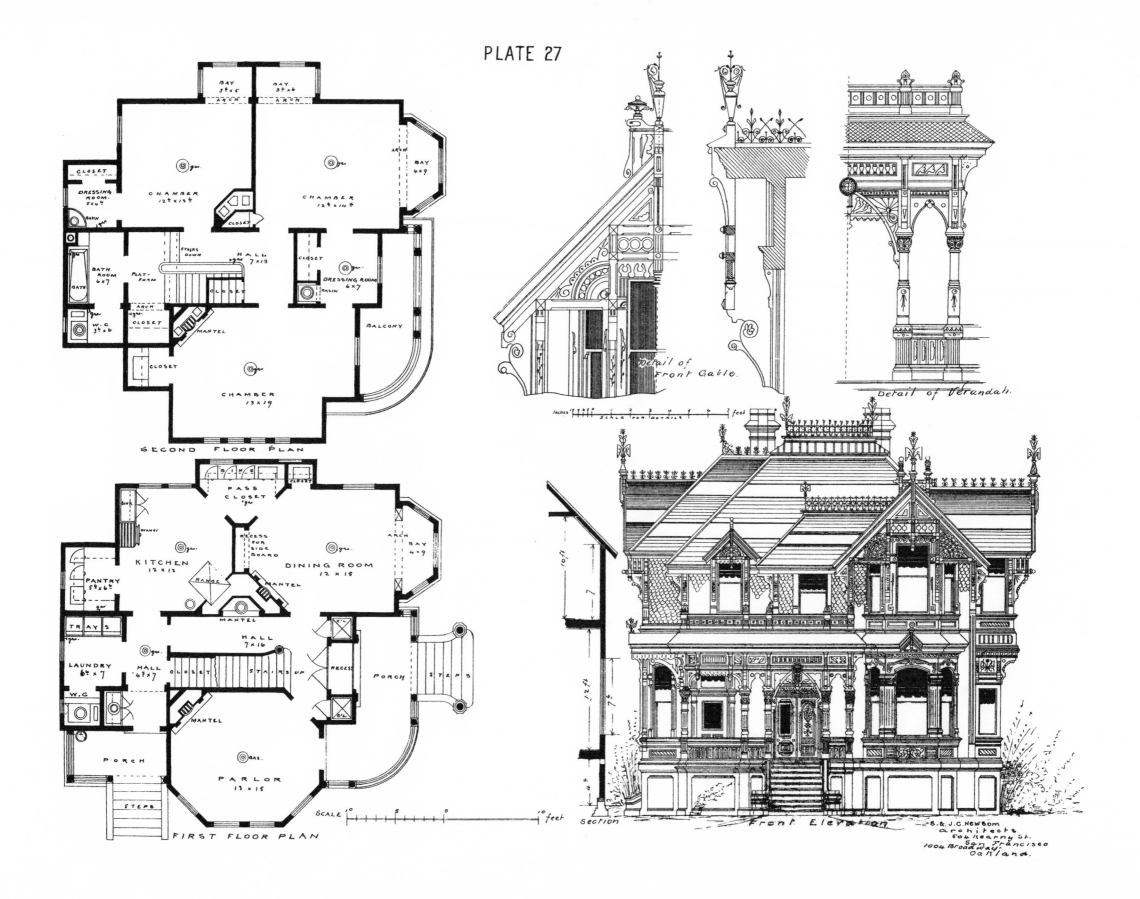

SECOND FLOOR PLAN

FIRST FLOOR PLAN

Detail of Front Gable.

Detail of Verandah.

Inches SCALE FOR DETAILS feet

SCALE 10 5 0 10 feet

Section

Front Elevation

B. & J. C. Newsom
architects
704 Kearny St.
San Francisco
1004 Broadway
Oakland.

W. J. ADAMS
WHOLESALE AND RETAIL DEALER IN
PUGET SOUND PINE AND ALL KINDS OF REDWOOD
LUMBER

Laths, Spars and Piles

Constantly on hand.

MILLS AT SEABECK, Washington Territory.

OFFICE AND YARD
Pier No. 17, Steuart Street, SAN FRANCISCO.

TELEPHONE NO. 820
BAY CITY IRON WORKS
C. L. BIGELOW, Proprietor,
MANUFACTURER OF

Wrought Iron Girders, Trusses, Crest Railings, Finials, Fences, Prison Cells, Iron Roofs, Weather Vanes, Gratings, etc.

GASOMETERS MANUFACTURED TO ORDER. BANK AND STORE FITTINGS.

323 MISSION STREET, and 103 and 105 FREMONT STREET, SAN FRANCISCO.

Estimates given and Iron Work furnished for Buildings.

◄ JAPANESE ⁑ WAX ⁑ FINISH ►
FOR PRESERVING AND CLEANING

Wood Carpets and Parquet Floors

Directions for Use on each Can. Price, $1.25 per Can.

A. C. DIETZ & CO.
SOLE AGENTS
9 Front Street - - - San Francisco.

ORION BROOKS, President. G. W. PEASE, Secretary.
ELECTRICAL SUPPLY CO.
Importers, Manufacturers and Dealers in
Telegraph and Telephone Supplies
Electric Bells and Electro-Medical Apparatus. Gear Cutting and Model Work to Order.

OFFICE AND WORKS:
328 BUSH STREET, - - - SAN FRANCISCO.
R. LANGER, Superintendent.

CALIFORNIA FURNITURE MANUFACTURING CO.
SUCCESSORS TO
N. P. COLE & CO.
MANUFACTURERS AND IMPORTERS
Furniture and Bedding
WOOD MANTELS
INTERIOR WOOD WORK AND HOUSE DECORATIONS A SPECIALTY.
224 and 226 Bush Street, San Francisco.

No. 333.

No. 313.

No. 328.

The First Brick Building with TERRA COTTA Trimmings erected in San Francisco.

ARCHITECTURAL TERRA COTTA.

SEWER AND CHIMNEY PIPE, ETC.

OFFICE OF
GLADDING, McBEAN & CO., 1358 & 1360 MARKET STREET.

No. 310.

No. 353.

No. 350.

WILLIAM McPHUN

Successor to HARTSHORN & McPHUN,

MANUFACTURER OF WINDOW SHADES

.CARPETS, OIL CLOTHS, PAPER HANGINGS, LINOLEUM, ETC.

861 MARKET STREET, OPPOSITE BALDWIN HOTEL, SAN FRANCISCO.

FACTORY: CORNER TWENTY-SECOND AND YORK STREETS.

WINDOW SHADES, for Dwelling Houses and Stores, a Specialty.

GOLDEN GATE PLASTER MILLS

215 and 217 Main Street,

BETWEEN HOWARD AND FOLSOM,   SAN FRANCISCO.

LUCAS & COMPANY,

MANUFACTURERS OF CALCINED PLASTER

(PLASTER OF PARIS)

Marble Dust, Land Plaster and Terra Alba.

BUSH & MALLETT

Gas and Oil Fixtures

JOBBING AND GAS FITTING.

PARTICULAR ATTENTION PAID TO JOBBING WORK OF ALL KINDS.

34 Geary Street, San Francisco.

FINE PLUMBING A SPECIALTY.

R. HERRING

Manufacturer of Fine Furniture

MANTELS, HOUSE, BANK & OFFICE FITTINGS

In Pacific Coast Woods, a Specialty,

DESIGNS FURNISHED.

Nos. 429 & 431 Fourth St., Corner Silver,

SAN FRANCISCO.

JOHN DOHERTY

Contractor and Builder

1604 JESSIE ST.

ESTIMATES GIVEN.

S. F. PIONEER VARNISH WORKS.

HUETER BROS. & CO.

Importers of Paints, Oils and Artists' Materials.

MANUFACTURERS OF   VARNISHES   COACH, CAR & FURNITURE

WORKS: Block 146, Potrero Nuevo, Bet. 23d and 24th Sts.   DEPOT: Corner Second and Market Sts.

SAN FRANCISCO.

SACK'S AUTOMATIC SELF-DISCHARGING

WATER CLOSET

The Only Self-Acting Tight-Seal Water Closet in the World!

Economy! Cleanliness! Health!

PERSONS ENGAGED IN

SANITARY ENTERPRISES,

ARCHITECTS,

Contractors and Builders,

ARE ESPECIALLY INVITED TO EXAMINE THE PRACTICAL WORKINGS OF

→* SACK'S *←

AUTOMATIC WATER CLOSET

Awarded FIRST PREMIUM at the MECHANICS' FAIR, held in San Francisco, 1882.

A written guarantee is given with each Closet that money will be returned, after a six months' trial, and any other Closet substituted in its place, if this Closet is not in the fullest sense, everything that is claimed for it.

It turns *every house* into a SANITARIUM, and is an assurance to those who trust it that neither *sewer gas* nor *noxious vapors* that invade our houses freighted with *disease* and *death*, shall enter. It is the invention of a Californian, and an Oakland enterprise.

Its merits surpass description, but a few prominent ones are mentioned below.

It is the only Self-Acting, Tight-Seal Water Closet in the World! It has no "*overflow*," rendering it a positive seal against *sewer gas* and reeking, noxious, poisonous vapors.

It is Cleanly, because it always presents a clean bowl. It rinses the bowl before and after each and every operation.

It is Self-Discharging. No notice to "pull the lever," "let on the water," etc., is necessary or proper.

A house in which it is in operation is free from the stench, the smell, the unhealthfulness of one in which other modern closets are in use.

It is Economical. It measures the water accurately, and uses, without variation, a similar amount at each and every operation. Not a drop but is utilized, thus dispensing with the superfluous amount that escapes unused by other closets, in order that their cumbrous and inefficient machinery may indifferently execute what has been ill conceived.

It is Scientific. Its action is governed by principle and under all degrees of pressure it works the same. A tan fifteen feet high obtains as ready and complete a response a one a thousand feet high.

It may be attached to a "main" with perfect impunity. N back suction, however strong, can draw from its seal a vestig of gas or a bubble of air. It holds in its bowl water as pur as when it left its font.

It is not a "water seal," nor does it depend on a "weight to effect its seal; but it derives its power from the suppl pipe, and combines it so as to fully accomplish this end:

Its simplicity, combining efficiency, renders the true aim perfect mechanical contrivances. It will effect for the chi all that the adult may desire in its use.

It is not high priced when compared with others. In th long run it is much cheaper. No "set-screws," "springs, "pans," or "pulls," to need repair or attention. Every a ticle used in its construction is of the best material and d signed to last.

As a sewer-flusher it is most effectual. In this regard has no equal. "Obstructions in the sewer" are rendered in probable, as the sudden discharge of water carries everythi before it

It is a water-economizer. It is impossible for the water escape it in a continuous stream, or for any length of time.

WHITTEMORE'S PATENT CHIMNEY.

W. E. STEVENS,

Sole Agent for San San Francisco,   **N. E. Cor. Larkin and Market Streets**

It will be a pleasure to demonstrate, to all who may favor me with a call, the practical workings of the most perfect Water Closet that has, as yet, been placed before the public.

PLATE 28

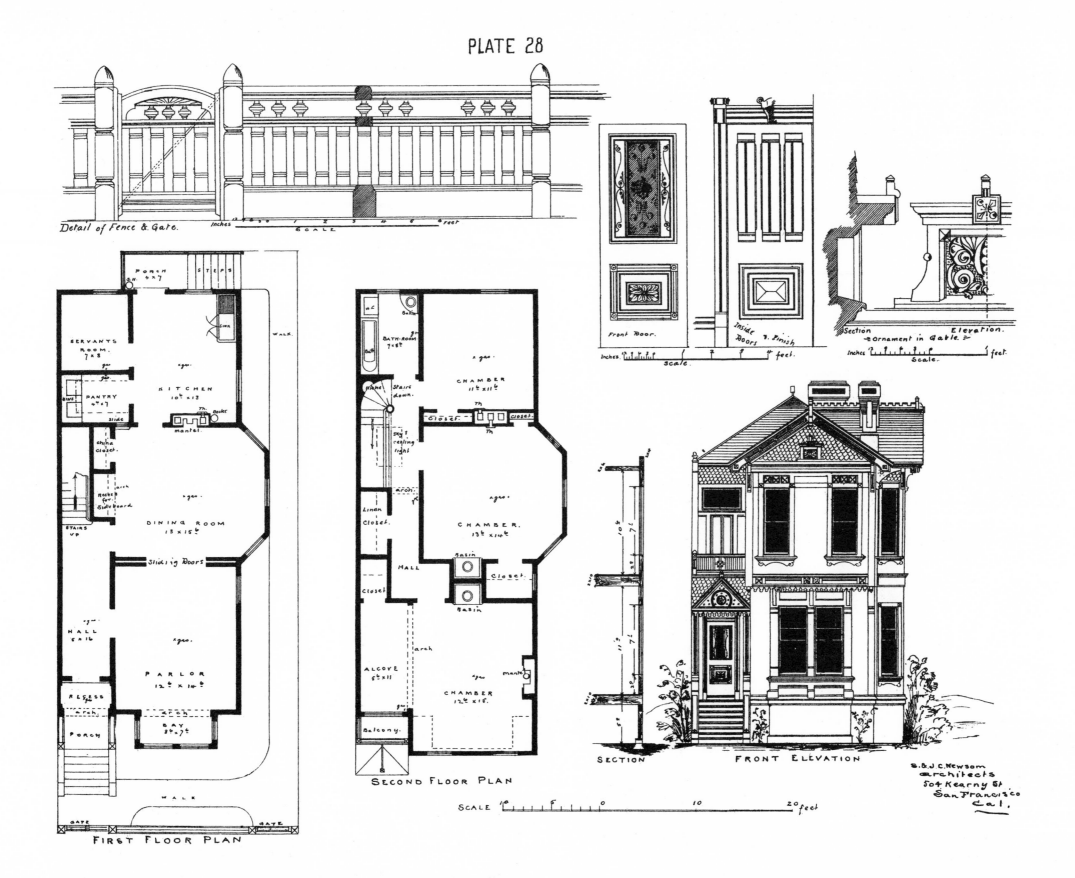

Detail of Fence & Gate.

Inches SCALE feet

Front Door.

Inside Doors & Finish.

Inches scale feet

Section Ornament in Gable. Elevation.

Inches Scale feet

FIRST FLOOR PLAN

SECOND FLOOR PLAN

SCALE 10 5 0 10 20 feet

SECTION

FRONT ELEVATION

S. & J. C. Newsom
Architects
504 Kearny St.
San Francisco
Cal.

PLATE 29

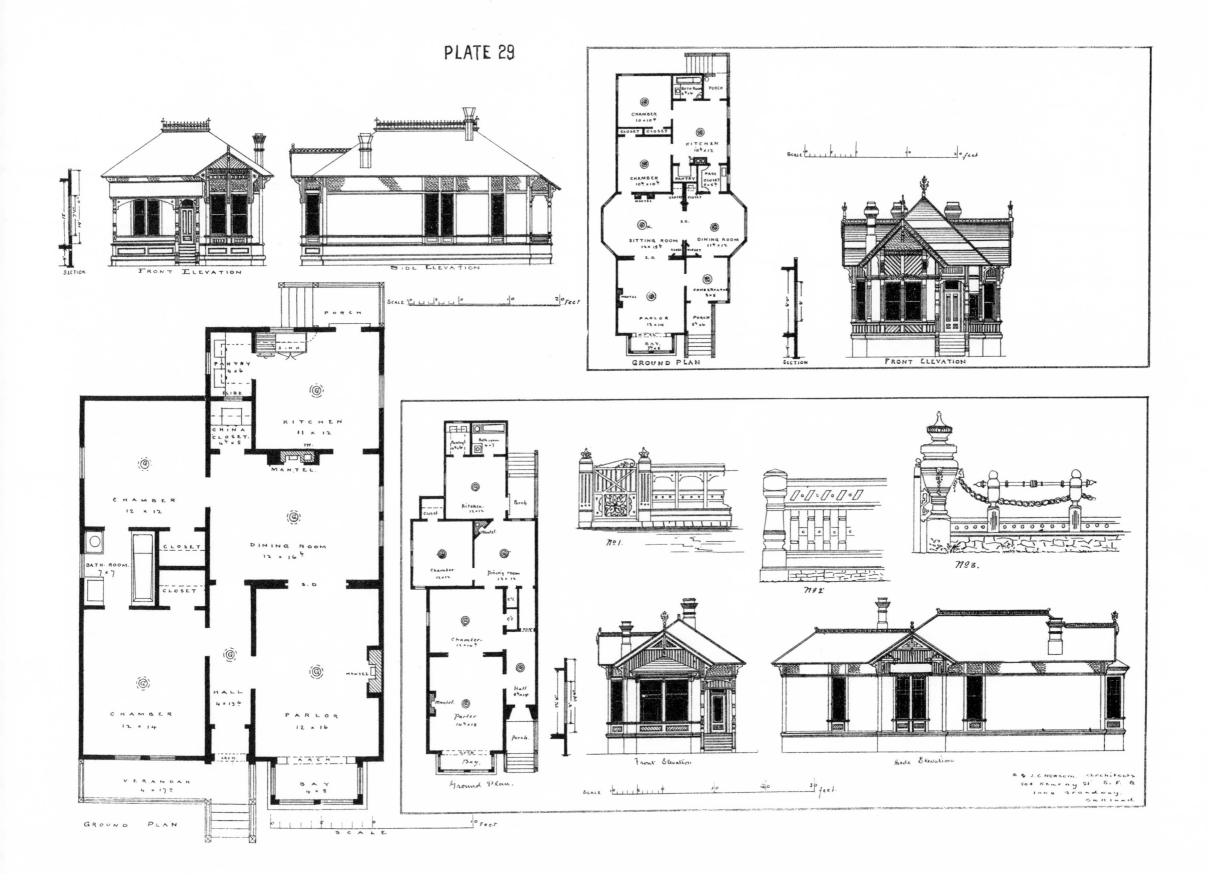

SECTION.

FRONT ELEVATION

SIDE ELEVATION

GROUND PLAN

SECTION

FRONT ELEVATION

SCALE

FRONT ELEVATION

SIDE ELEVATION

GROUND PLAN

SCALE

GROUND PLAN

PLATE 30

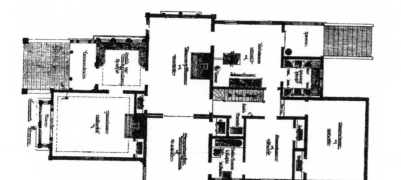

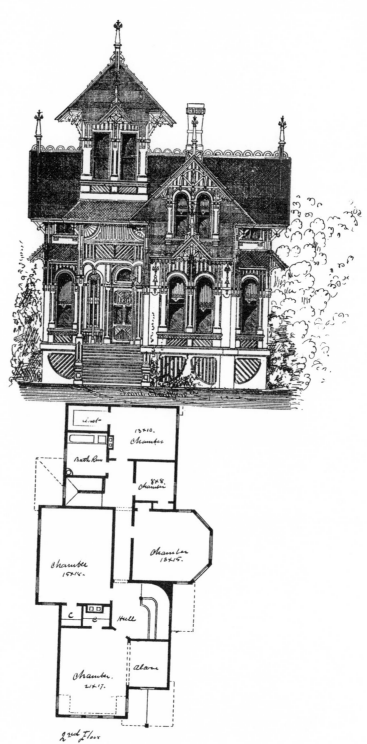

Front Elevation

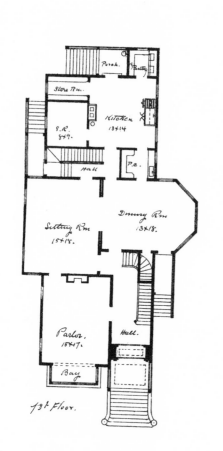

1st Floor.

Section

Front Elevation

2nd Floor.

J. & C. Newsom
archts.

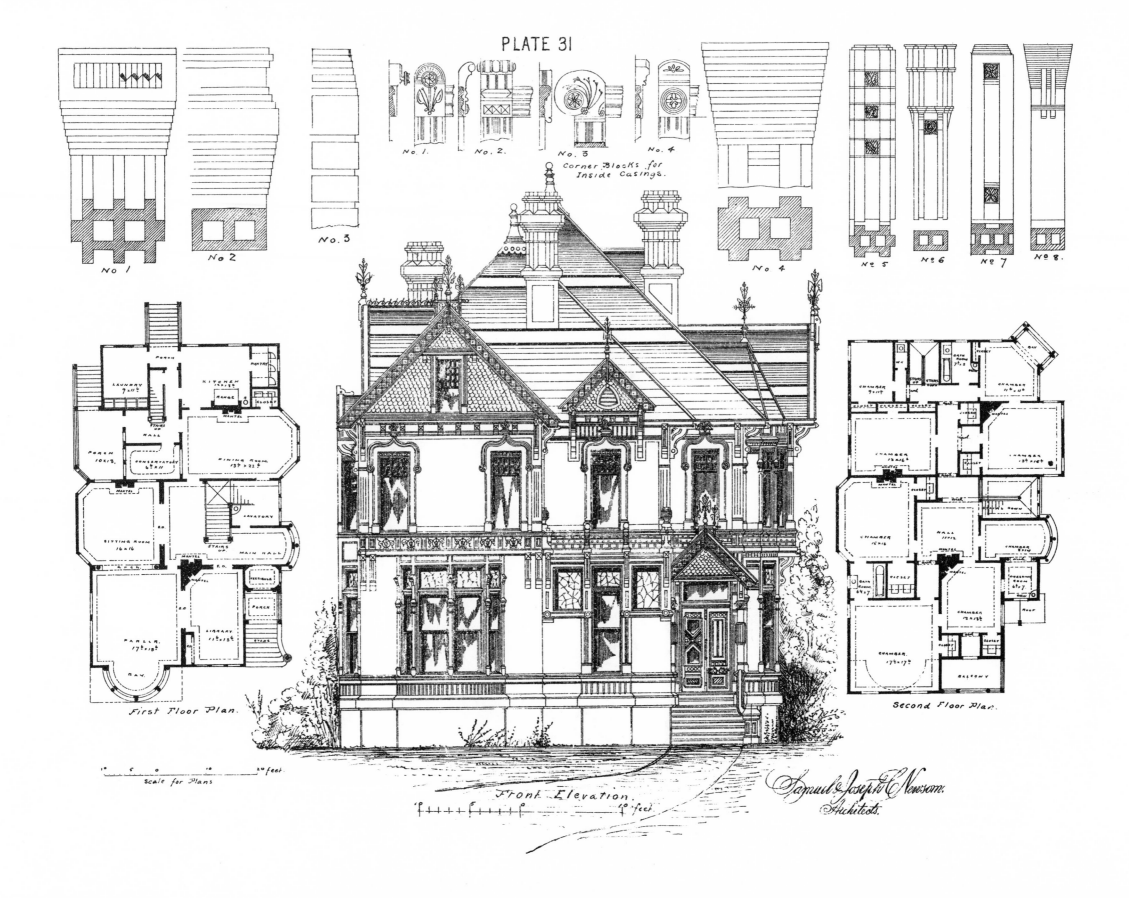

PLATE 31

No. 1. No. 2. No. 3. No. 4.
Corner Blocks for
Inside Casings.

No 1 No 2 No. 3 No 4 N° 5 N° 6 N° 7 N° 8.

First Floor Plan.

Scale for Plans

Front Elevation.

Second Floor Plan.

Samuel & Joseph C. Newsom.
Architects.

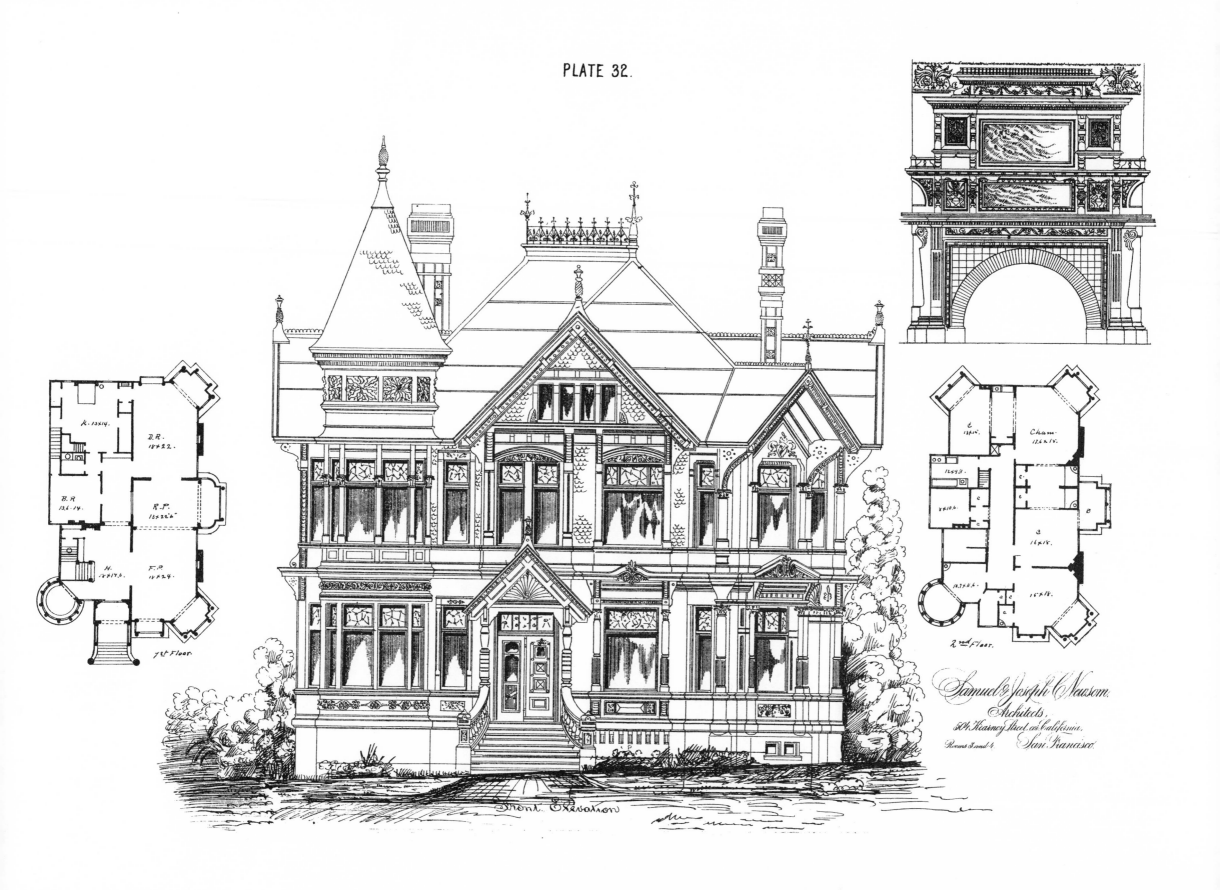

PLATE 32.

Front Elevation

1st Floor.

2nd Floor.

Samuel & Joseph C. Newsom.
Architects,
504 Kearney Street cor. California.
Rooms 3 and 4.   San Francisco.

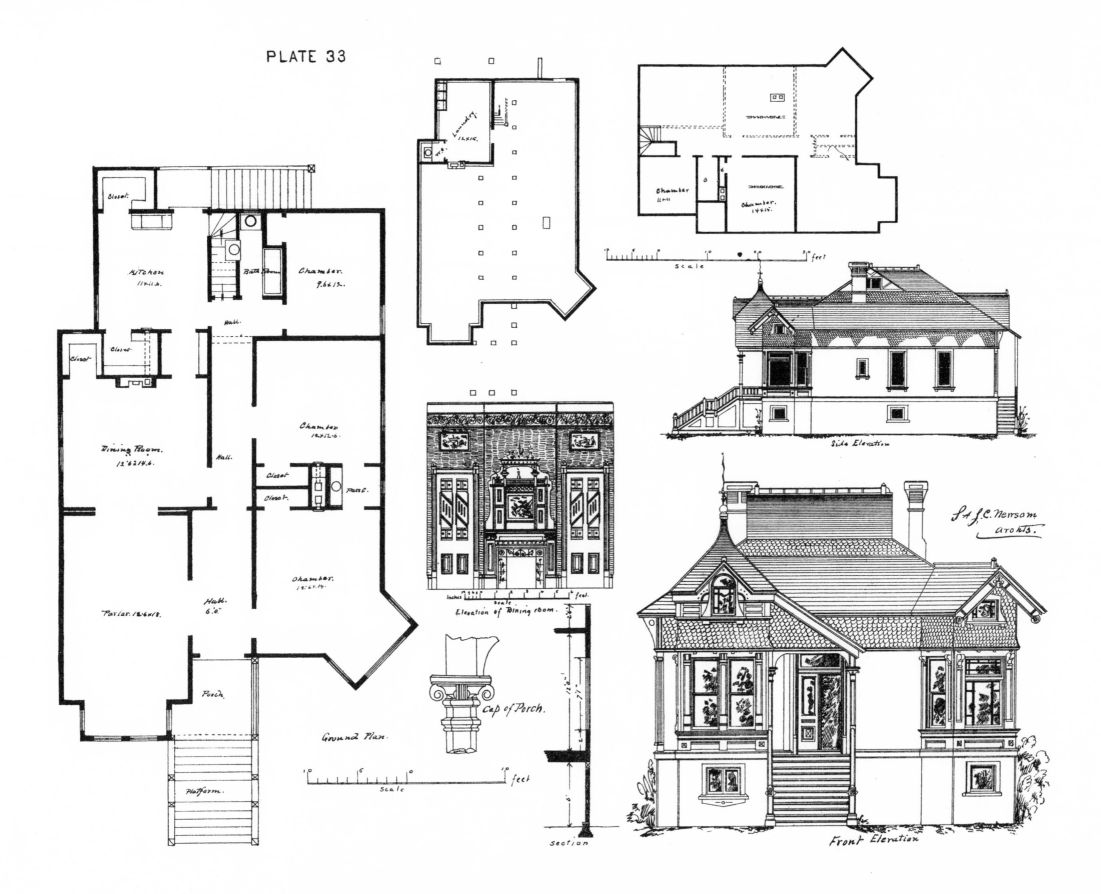

PLATE 33

Closet.

Kitchen
11 x 11.6

Bath Room

Chamber.
9.6 x 12.

Hall.

Closet.

Closet.

Dining Room.
12.6 x 14.6

Hall.

Chamber
12 x 12.6

Closet

Closet

Pass.

Chamber
12.6 x 14.

Parlor. 12.6 x 18.

Hall.
6.0

Porch.

Platform.

Ground Plan.

Laundry
12 x 15.

Chamber
14 x 11

Chamber
14 x 15.

Scale

Elevation of Dining room.

Inches   Scale   feet

Cap of Porch.

Section

Scale   feet

Side Elevation

S. A. J. C. Newsom
Archts.

Front Elevation

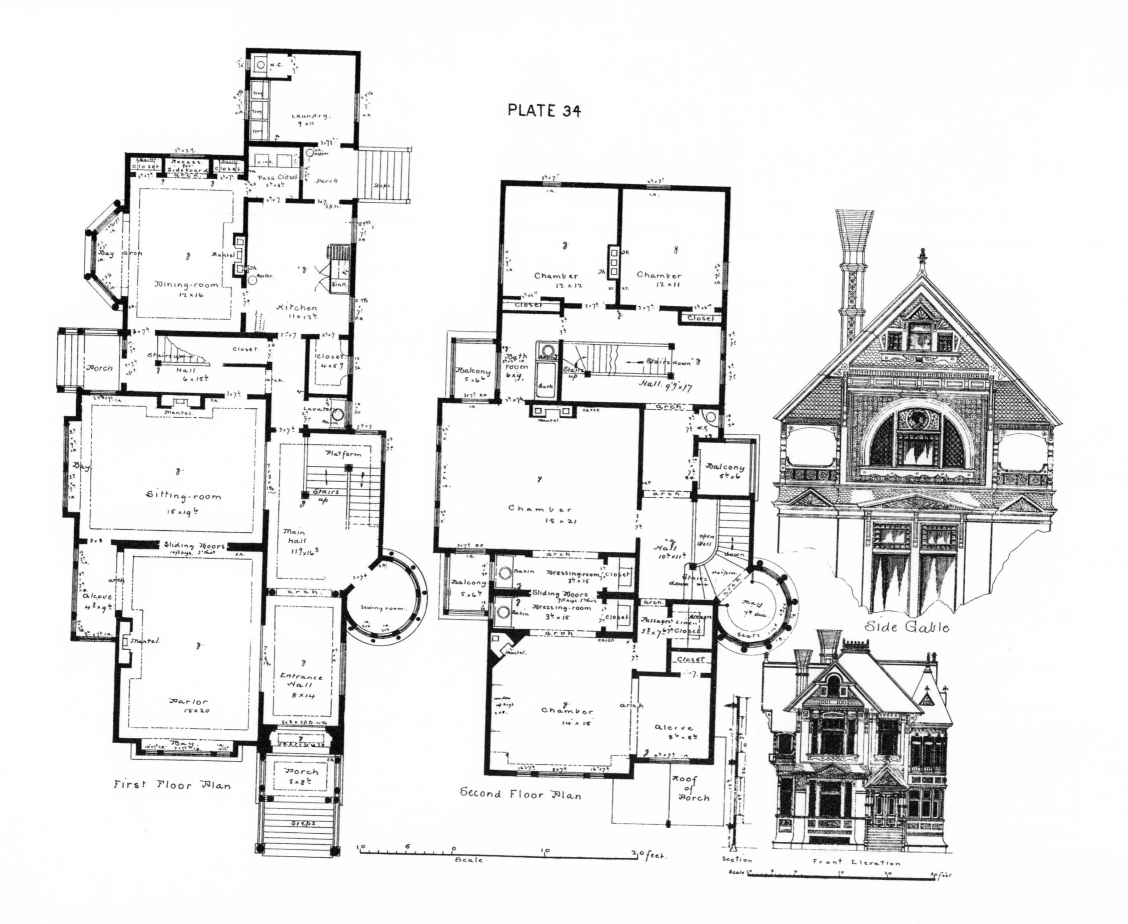

PLATE 34

First Floor Plan

Second Floor Plan

Side Gable

Front Elevation

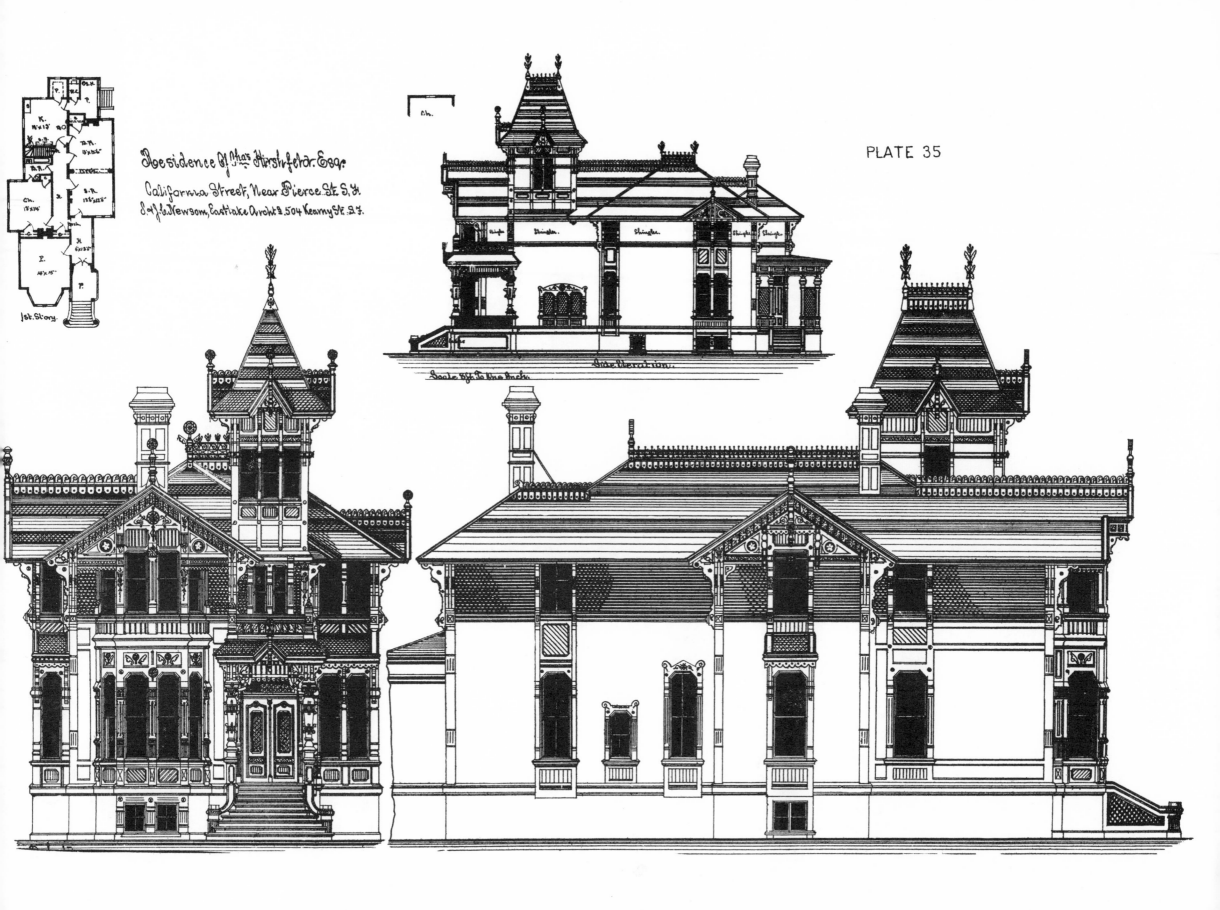

Residence of Chas. Hirschfeld. Esq.

California Street, Near Pierce St. S. F.

S. & J. C. Newsom, Eastlake Archt's. 504 Kearny St. S. F.

1st. Story.

PLATE 35

Scale 8ft. To One Inch.

Side Elevation.

Here are the designs for some of California's most fanciful Victorian houses, presented as originally published in a book for the carpenter-builder. Much nineteenth-century domestic architecture, whether for prospective homeowners or the speculative investor, resulted from just such *pattern books*, which remain as invaluable treasuries of the wide variety of design forms and styles in use at the time. This is a facsimile of an unusually rare volume (only a few copies are known to exist) published by Samuel and Joseph Cather Newsom, the architects of the famous Carson house in Eureka. The Newsoms were responsible for many of the Victorian delights in San Francisco and throughout California. Working flamboyantly with styles ranging from Eastlake through Queen Anne to late Shingle and Craftsman, they marked all their creations with a distinctive imprint, a playful, even outrageous maneuvering and mixing of images into overall designs that from both a visual and practical point of view ultimately work.

The 35 plates in this volume contain side elevations, floor plans and details for 37 dwellings of various sizes. Nineteen of these were for homes actually built; the remainder were probably intended as workable plans either for individual use or for "spec" housing. Although builders could buy more complete sets of drawings from architectural firms, in most cases they found it sufficient to work from the scale drawings in pattern books such as this. For bibliophiles and buffs of Victoriana, the entire volume has been reproduced in its original size, including all of the advertisement pages. An added introduction by noted architectural historian David Gebhard gives recently uncovered details about the Newsoms and their publications together with an evaluation of their work.

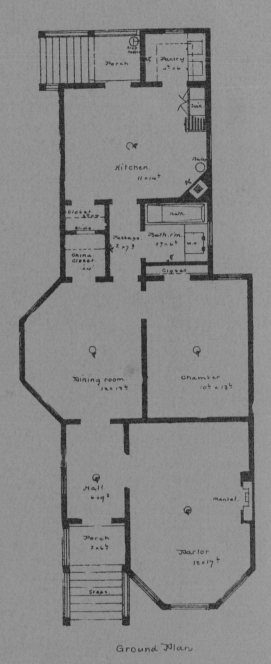

Ground Plan.

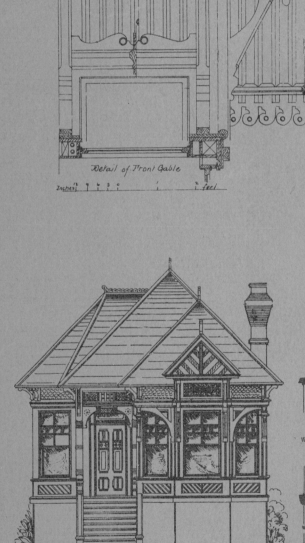

Detail of Front Gable

Front Elevation.

Section.

Side Elevation.

1330 1896 4
11•13•00 6 MAB

3 1430 02618408 7

a31430026184087b
UNIV. OF MD. COLLEGE PARK

7559

NTHP. HQ — L

DO NOT CIRCULATE